IRISH PUB

Publications International, Ltd.

Microwave Cooking: Microwave ovens vary in wattage. Use the cooking times as guidelines and check for doneness before adding more time.

Let's get social!
⊙ @Publications_International
🛇 @PublicationsInternational
www.pilbooks.com

Sage-Roasted Pork with Rutabaga
(page 76)

Irish Stout Chicken
(page 95)

CONTENTS

Potato and Corned Beef Cakes

MAKES 10 CAKES

- 2 pounds russet potatoes, divided
- 2 teaspoons salt, divided
- 6 tablespoons all-purpose flour
- ¼ cup whole milk
- 1 egg, beaten
- ½ teaspoon black pepper
- 1 cup chopped corned beef (leftover or deli corned beef, about ⅓ pound), cut into ¼-inch pieces
- 1 tablespoon butter
- 1 tablespoon olive oil
- Chopped fresh parsley (optional)

1 Peel half of potatoes; cut into 1-inch pieces. Place in medium saucepan; add 1 teaspoon salt and water to cover by 2 inches. Bring to a simmer over medium heat; cook 15 minutes or until tender. Drain potatoes; rice into medium bowl.

2 Peel remaining half of potatoes; grate with box grater. Squeeze out and discard liquid from grated potatoes. Add grated potatoes to riced potatoes in bowl; stir in flour, milk, egg, remaining 1 teaspoon salt and pepper. Stir in corned beef until well blended.

3 Heat butter and oil in large skillet (preferably cast iron) over medium heat. Shape ⅓ cupfuls of potato mixture into patties; cook in batches 3 to 4 minutes per side or until golden brown. (Do not crowd patties in skillet.) Sprinkle with parsley, if desired.

Lamb and Mint Hand Pies

MAKES 8 APPETIZER SERVINGS

2 cups plus 1 tablespoon all-purpose flour, divided

1 teaspoon salt, divided

10 tablespoons cold butter, cut into small pieces

7 to 8 tablespoons ice water

1 pound ground lamb

1 small onion, finely chopped

1 carrot, finely chopped

½ cup beef broth

1 teaspoon Dijon mustard

¼ teaspoon black pepper

1 tablespoon chopped fresh mint

½ cup (2 ounces) shredded Irish Cheddar cheese

1 egg, lightly beaten

1 Combine 2 cups flour and ½ teaspoon salt in medium bowl. Cut in butter with pastry blender or two knives until mixture resembles coarse crumbs. Add water, 1 tablespoon at a time, stirring with fork until loose dough forms. Knead dough in bowl 1 to 2 times until it comes together. Divide dough into four pieces; press each into 4-inch disc. Wrap dough with plastic wrap; freeze 15 minutes.

2 Meanwhile, heat large skillet over medium-high heat. Add lamb; cook 7 to 8 minutes or until lightly browned, stirring occasionally. Drain well; remove to plate. Add onion and carrot to skillet; cook 2 to 3 minutes or until vegetables begin to soften, stirring occasionally. Stir in lamb; cook 1 minute. Add remaining 1 tablespoon flour; cook and stir 1 minute. Add broth, mustard, remaining ½ teaspoon salt and pepper; cook over medium heat 2 minutes or until thickened. Remove from heat; stir in mint. Cool 10 minutes. Stir in cheese.

3 Preheat oven to 400°F. Line large baking sheet with parchment paper or spray with nonstick cooking spray.

4 Working with one disc at a time, roll out dough into 9-inch circle on lightly floured surface. Cut out four circles with 4-inch round cookie cutter (16 circles total). Place eight circles on prepared baking sheet. Top each with one eighth of lamb filling, leaving ½-inch border around edge of circle. Top with remaining dough circles, pressing edges to seal. Press edges again with tines of fork. Brush tops with egg; cut 1-inch slit in top of each pie with tip of knife.

5 Bake 28 to 30 minutes or until golden brown. Serve hot or at room temperature.

Beet and Goat Cheese Salad

MAKES 4 SERVINGS

1 pound whole beets with greens
3 quarts water
2⅛ teaspoons salt, divided
Mixed greens (optional)
2 tablespoons red wine vinegar

1 teaspoon Dijon mustard
¼ teaspoon black pepper
¼ cup extra virgin olive oil
¼ cup canola or vegetable oil
½ cup chopped hazelnuts
4 ounces goat cheese

1 Cut off beet greens; set aside. Bring water and 2 teaspoons salt to a boil in large saucepan. Add beets; cook 20 to 25 minutes or until crisp-tender. Drain beets; peel under running water to help prevent staining fingers. Cut each beet into eight pieces. Place in large bowl.

2 Thoroughly wash beet greens; remove and discard tough stems. Tear greens into large pieces. Add mixed greens, if necessary, to make 6 cups. Add greens to bowl with beets.

3 For dressing, whisk vinegar, mustard, pepper and remaining ⅛ teaspoon salt in medium bowl until blended. Slowly drizzle in olive oil and canola oil, whisking constantly.

4 Toast hazelnuts in small skillet over medium heat 5 minutes or until golden brown. Transfer to medium bowl; cool slightly. Stir in goat cheese. Shape teaspoonfuls of cheese mixture into balls. Toss beets and greens with dressing; top with cheese balls.

Tip
The beets, dressing and cheese balls can
all be prepared in advance. Assemble
the salad just before serving.

Sausage Rolls

MAKES 4 SERVINGS

8 ounces ground pork

¼ cup finely chopped onion

½ teaspoon coarse salt

1 teaspoon minced garlic

½ teaspoon dried thyme

½ teaspoon dried basil

¼ teaspoon dried marjoram

¼ teaspoon black pepper

1 sheet frozen puff pastry (half of 17-ounce package), thawed

1 egg, beaten

1 Preheat oven to 400°F. Line large baking sheet with parchment paper.

2 Combine pork, onion, salt, garlic, thyme, basil, marjoram and pepper in medium bowl; mix well.

3 Place puff pastry on floured surface; cut lengthwise into three strips at seams. Roll each third into 10×4½-inch rectangle. Shape one third of pork mixture into 10-inch log; arrange log along top edge of one pastry rectangle. Brush bottom ½ inch of rectangle with egg. Roll pastry down around pork; press to seal. Cut each roll crosswise into four pieces; place seam side down on prepared baking sheet. Repeat with remaining puff pastry and pork mixture. Brush top of each roll with egg.

4 Bake 5 minutes or until sausage is cooked through and pastry is golden brown and puffed. Remove to wire rack to cool 10 minutes. Serve warm.

Crispy Smashed Potatoes

MAKES ABOUT 6 SERVINGS

1 tablespoon plus ½ teaspoon salt, divided

3 pounds unpeeled small red potatoes (2 inches or smaller)

4 tablespoons (½ stick) butter, melted, divided

¼ teaspoon black pepper

½ cup grated Parmesan cheese (optional)

1 Fill large saucepan three-fourths full of water; add 1 tablespoon salt. Bring to a boil over high heat. Add potatoes; boil 20 minutes or until potatoes are tender when pierced with tip of sharp knife. Drain potatoes; set aside until cool enough to handle.

2 Preheat oven to 450°F. Brush baking sheet with 2 tablespoons butter. Working with one potato at a time, smash with hand or bottom of measuring cup to about ½-inch thickness. Arrange smashed potatoes in single layer on prepared baking sheet. Brush with remaining 2 tablespoons butter; sprinkle with remaining ½ teaspoon salt and pepper.

3 Bake 30 to 40 minutes or until bottoms of potatoes are golden brown. Turn potatoes; bake 10 minutes. Sprinkle with cheese, if desired; bake 5 minutes or until cheese is melted.

Roasted Garlic & Stout Mac & Cheese

MAKES 8 TO 10 SERVINGS

6 tablespoons (¾ stick) butter, divided, plus additional for baking dish
1 head garlic
1 tablespoon olive oil
1¼ teaspoons salt, divided
1 cup panko bread crumbs
¼ cup all-purpose flour
½ teaspoon black pepper

2 cups whole milk
¾ cup Irish stout
2 cups (8 ounces) shredded sharp Cheddar cheese
2 cups (8 ounces) shredded Dubliner cheese
1 pound cellentani pasta,* cooked and drained

Or substitute elbow macaroni, penne or other favorite pasta shape.

1 Preheat oven to 375°F. Butter 4-quart shallow baking dish.

2 Place garlic on 10-inch piece of foil; drizzle with oil and crimp shut. Place on small baking sheet; bake 30 minutes or until tender. Cool 15 minutes; squeeze cloves into small bowl. Mash into smooth paste.

3 Microwave 2 tablespoons butter in medium bowl until melted. Stir in ¼ teaspoon salt until dissolved. Stir in panko until well blended.

4 Melt remaining 4 tablespoons butter in large saucepan over medium heat. Add flour; cook and stir until lightly browned. Stir in roasted garlic paste, remaining 1 teaspoon salt and pepper. Slowly whisk in milk and stout. Simmer until thickened, whisking constantly. Remove from heat; whisk in cheeses, ½ cup at a time, until melted. Combine cheese mixture and pasta in large bowl. Spoon into prepared baking dish; sprinkle with panko mixture.

5 Bake 40 minutes or until bubbly and topping is golden brown. Let stand 10 minutes before serving.

Potato Cakes with Brussels Sprouts

MAKES 12 CAKES

2½ pounds Yukon Gold potatoes, peeled and cut into 1-inch cubes

6 tablespoons (¾ stick) butter, melted

⅓ cup milk, warmed

2 teaspoons salt

½ teaspoon black pepper

3 tablespoons vegetable oil, divided

12 ounces Brussels sprouts, ends trimmed, thinly sliced

4 green onions, thinly sliced on the diagonal

1 Place potatoes in large saucepan or Dutch oven; add cold water to cover by 2 inches. Bring to a boil over high heat. Reduce heat to medium-low; cover and simmer 10 minutes or until potatoes are tender. Drain.

2 Return potatoes to saucepan; mash with potato masher until slightly chunky. Stir in butter, milk, salt and pepper until well blended; set aside.

3 Heat 1 tablespoon oil in large nonstick skillet over medium-high heat. Add Brussels sprouts; cook 8 minutes or until tender and lightly browned, stirring occasionally. Stir Brussels sprouts and green onions into potato mixture. Wipe out skillet with paper towel.

4 Heat 1 tablespoon oil in skillet over medium heat. Drop potato mixture into skillet by ½ cupfuls, spacing about ½ inch apart. (Use spoon to remove mixture from cup if necessary.) Cook 3 minutes per side or until cakes are browned and crisp, pressing down lightly with spatula. Transfer to platter; tent with foil to keep warm. Repeat with remaining 1 tablespoon oil and potato mixture.

Rhubarb Chutney

MAKES ABOUT 2 CUPS

1 cup coarsely chopped
    peeled apple

½ cup sugar

¼ cup water

¼ cup dark raisins

1 teaspoon grated lemon peel

2 cups sliced fresh rhubarb
    (½-inch pieces)

3 tablespoons coarsely
    chopped pecans

2 to 3 teaspoons white
    vinegar

¾ teaspoon ground cinnamon
    (optional)

1 Combine apple, sugar, water, raisins and lemon peel in medium
saucepan; heat over medium heat until sugar is dissolved, stirring
constantly. Reduce heat to low; cook, uncovered, 5 minutes or until
apple is almost tender.

2 Stir in rhubarb and pecans; bring to a boil over high heat. Reduce
heat to low; cook 8 to 10 minutes or until slightly thickened, stirring
occasionally. Stir in vinegar and cinnamon, if desired, during last
2 to 3 minutes of cooking.

3 Remove from heat; cool to room temperature. Cover; refrigerate until
ready to serve. Serve with cheese and crackers.

Potted Beer and Cheddar
MAKES ABOUT 3 CUPS

8 ounces cream cheese, softened

4 tablespoons CABOT® Unsalted Butter, softened

4 cups grated CABOT® Sharp Cheddar (about 1 pound)

1 tablespoon minced fresh chives

1 tablespoon chopped fresh parsley

1 teaspoon Worcestershire sauce

1 teaspoon Dijon mustard

1 teaspoon prepared horseradish

½ clove garlic, minced

¼ teaspoon ground black pepper

2 to 3 drops hot pepper sauce

¼ to ½ cup flat beer

1 With electric mixer, beat together cream cheese and butter until well blended. Mix in cheese.

2 Mix in all remaining ingredients except beer. Add enough beer to make spread of desired consistency (mixture will thicken further after chilling).

3 Pack into earthenware crock or other ceramic dish; cover and refrigerate for several hours to allow flavors to blend. Serve with apple slices and dark rye bread or crackers.

Note
Spread can be made several days in advance.

Beef and Beer Sliders

MAKES 12 SLIDERS

6 tablespoons ketchup

2 tablespoons mayonnaise

2 teaspoons Dijon mustard

1½ pounds ground beef

½ cup beer

1 teaspoon salt

½ teaspoon garlic powder

½ teaspoon onion powder

½ teaspoon ground cumin

½ teaspoon dried oregano

¼ teaspoon black pepper

3 slices sharp Cheddar cheese, cut into 4 pieces

12 slider buns or potato dinner rolls

12 baby lettuce leaves

12 plum tomato slices

1 Combine ketchup, mayonnaise and mustard in small bowl; set aside.

2 Combine beef, beer, salt, garlic powder, onion powder, cumin, oregano and pepper in medium bowl. Shape mixture into 12 (¼-inch-thick) patties.

3 Prepare grill for direct cooking over medium-high heat. Spray grid with nonstick cooking spray. Add half of patties; grill 2 minutes. Turn; top each with 1 piece cheese. Grill 2 minutes or until cheese is melted and patties are cooked through. Remove to large plate; keep warm. Repeat with remaining patties and cheese.

4 Serve sliders on rolls with ketchup mixture, lettuce and tomato.

Beer Pretzels

MAKES 12 PRETZELS

¼ cup warm water
1 package (¼ ounce) active dry yeast
1 tablespoon sugar
1 tablespoon olive oil
1 teaspoon kosher salt, divided
1 cup brown ale, at room temperature

3¾ to 4 cups all-purpose flour
2 cups hot water
1 teaspoon baking soda
1 egg, well beaten
2 tablespoons butter, melted
Mustard (optional)

1 Place warm water in large bowl; sprinkle with yeast. Let stand 5 minutes or until mixture is bubbly. Add sugar, oil, ¾ teaspoon salt, ale and 3¾ cups flour; stir to form soft dough. Knead on floured surface 6 to 8 minutes or until smooth and elastic, adding additional flour by tablespoonfuls if necessary.

2 Place dough in greased medium bowl; turn to grease top. Cover; let rise in warm place 45 minutes or until doubled in size.

3 Punch down dough. Divide into 12 pieces. Roll each piece into a rope about 20 inches long. If dough becomes too difficult to roll, let stand 10 minutes. Shape ropes into pretzels.

4 Preheat oven to 425°F. Line baking sheet with parchment paper or spray with nonstick cooking spray. Stir hot water into baking soda in pie plate until blended. Dip pretzels into mixture; place on prepared baking sheet. Cover loosely and let stand in warm place 15 to 20 minutes. Brush pretzels with egg; sprinkle with remaining ¼ teaspoon salt.

5 Bake 10 minutes or until golden brown. Brush pretzels with melted butter. Serve with mustard, if desired.

Variation

Sprinkle a small amount of cheese over pretzels before baking—Parmesan, Asiago or Cheddar are good choices. Or add ½ cup (2 ounces) Cheddar cheese to batter when you are almost finished kneading in step 1.

Beet and Arugula Salad

MAKES 6 TO 8 SERVINGS

8 medium beets (5 to
    6 ounces each)

⅓ cup red wine vinegar

¾ teaspoon salt

½ teaspoon black pepper

3 tablespoons extra virgin
    olive oil

1 package (5 ounces) baby
    arugula

1 package (4 ounces) goat
    cheese with garlic and
    herbs, crumbled

1 Place beets in large saucepan; add water to cover by 2 inches. Bring to a boil over medium-high heat. Reduce heat to medium-low; cover and simmer 30 minutes or until beets can be easily pierced with tip of knife. Drain well; set aside until cool enough to handle.

2 Meanwhile, whisk vinegar, salt and pepper in large bowl. Slowly add oil in thin steady stream, whisking until well blended. Remove 3 tablespoons dressing to medium bowl.

3 Peel beets and cut into wedges. Add warm beets to large bowl; toss to coat with dressing. Add arugula to medium bowl; toss gently to coat with dressing. Place arugula on platter or plates, top with beets and cheese.

Scotch Eggs

MAKES 8 SERVINGS

10 eggs, divided
2 tablespoons vegetable oil
1½ cups panko bread crumbs
1 pound bulk breakfast sausage

¼ cup thinly sliced green onions
¾ cup all-purpose flour
2 tablespoons whole grain mustard

1 Preheat oven to 400°F. Line large baking sheet with foil.

2 Place 8 eggs in large saucepan filled with cold water; cover and bring to a boil over medium-high heat. Turn off heat; let stand 10 minutes. Run eggs under cool water to stop cooking. When cool enough to handle, carefully crack and peel eggs.

3 Meanwhile, heat oil in medium skillet over medium heat. Add panko; cook 8 minutes or until toasted and golden brown, stirring occasionally. Remove to medium bowl; let cool.

4 Combine sausage and green onions in medium bowl. Place flour in shallow bowl. Lightly beat remaining 2 eggs and mustard in another shallow bowl.

5 Scoop out one eighth of sausage mixture; press flat in palm of your hand. Place 1 cooked egg in center of mixture and wrap sausage around it. Gently roll between your hands until sausage completely encloses egg. Coat sausage-wrapped egg with flour, shaking off excess. Dip in egg-mustard mixture; roll in panko to coat. Place on prepared baking sheet. Repeat with remaining eggs and sausage.

6 Bake 16 to 18 minutes or until sausage is cooked through. Drain well on paper towel-lined plate. Serve immediately.

Irish Soda Bread

MAKES 12 SERVINGS

2½ cups all-purpose flour
1¼ cups whole wheat flour
1 cup currants
¼ cup sugar
4 teaspoons baking powder
2 teaspoons caraway seeds (optional)

1 teaspoon salt
½ teaspoon baking soda
½ cup (1 stick) butter, cut into small pieces
1⅓ to 1½ cups buttermilk

1 Preheat oven to 350°F. Line baking sheet with parchment paper or spray with nonstick cooking spray.

2 Combine all-purpose flour, whole wheat flour, currants, sugar, baking powder, caraway seeds, if desired, salt and baking soda in large bowl.

3 Cut in butter with pastry blender or two knives until mixture resembles coarse crumbs. Add buttermilk; mix until slightly sticky dough forms. Transfer dough to prepared baking sheet; shape into 8-inch round.

4 Bake 50 to 60 minutes or until bread is golden brown and crust is firm. Cool on baking sheet 10 minutes; remove to wire rack to cool completely.

Boxty Cakes

MAKES 4 SERVINGS (16 TO 20 PANCAKES)

2 medium russet potatoes
   (1 pound), peeled, divided
⅔ cup all-purpose flour
1 teaspoon baking powder

½ teaspoon salt
⅔ cup buttermilk
3 tablespoons butter

1 Cut 1 potato into 1-inch chunks; place in small saucepan and add cold water to cover by 2 inches. Bring to a boil over medium-high heat; cook 14 to 18 minutes or until tender. Drain potato; return to saucepan and mash. Transfer to medium bowl.

2 Grate remaining potato on large holes of box grater; add to bowl with mashed potato. Stir in flour, baking powder and salt until blended. Stir in buttermilk.

3 Melt 1 tablespoon butter in large nonstick skillet over medium heat. Drop four slightly heaping tablespoonfuls of batter into skillet; flatten into 2½-inch circles. Cook 4 minutes per side or until golden and puffed. Remove to plate; cover to keep warm. Repeat with remaining batter and butter. Serve immediately.

Serving Suggestion

Serve with melted butter, sour cream or maple syrup.

Double Pea Soup

MAKES 6 SERVINGS

1 tablespoon vegetable oil
1 onion, finely chopped
3 cloves garlic, minced
6 cups water
2 cups dried split peas
1 bay leaf

1 teaspoon ground mustard
1½ cups frozen green peas
1 teaspoon salt
¼ teaspoon black pepper
Sour cream (optional)

1 Heat oil in large saucepan or Dutch oven over medium-high heat. Add onion; cook 5 minutes or until tender, stirring occasionally. Add garlic; cook and stir 1 minute.

2 Add water, split peas, bay leaf and mustard; bring to a boil over high heat. Reduce heat to medium-low; cover and simmer 45 minutes or until split peas are tender, stirring occasionally.

3 Stir in green peas, salt and pepper; cover and simmer 10 minutes or until green peas are tender. Remove and discard bay leaf. Working in batches, blend soup in blender or food processor until smooth.

4 Top each serving with sour cream, if desired.

Note
For a smoky flavor, add a chipotle pepper
during the last 5 minutes of cooking.

Irish Lamb Stew

MAKES 8 SERVINGS

½ cup all-purpose flour

2 teaspoons salt, divided

½ teaspoon black pepper, divided

3 pounds boneless lamb stew meat, cut into 1½-inch cubes

3 tablespoons vegetable oil

1 cup chopped onion

1 can (about 15 ounces) Irish stout, divided

1 teaspoon sugar

1 teaspoon dried thyme

1 pound unpeeled small new potatoes, quartered

1 pound carrots, peeled and cut into ½-inch pieces

½ cup water

1 cup frozen peas

¼ cup chopped fresh parsley

1 Combine flour, 1 teaspoon salt and ¼ teaspoon pepper in large bowl. Add lamb; toss to coat, shaking off excess. Discard any remaining flour mixture.

2 Heat oil in Dutch oven over medium heat. Cook lamb in batches 7 minutes or until browned on all sides. Remove to bowl.

3 Add onion and ¼ cup stout to Dutch oven; cook 10 minutes, scraping up browned bits from bottom of pan. Return lamb to Dutch oven; stir in remaining stout, 1 teaspoon salt, ¼ teaspoon pepper, sugar and thyme. If necessary, add enough water so liquid just covers lamb. Bring to a boil over medium-high heat. Reduce heat to low; cover and simmer 1½ hours or until lamb is tender.

4 Stir in potatoes, carrots and ½ cup water; cover and cook 30 minutes or until vegetables are tender. Stir in peas and parsley; cook 5 to 10 minutes or until heated through.

Cock-A-Leekie Soup

MAKES 6 TO 8 SERVINGS

4 cups chicken broth

4 cups water

2½ pounds chicken thighs (with bones and skin)

3 stalks celery, sliced

2 bay leaves

5 to 6 large leeks (about 2½ pounds)

½ cup uncooked pearl barley

1 teaspoon salt

1 teaspoon ground allspice

12 pitted prunes, halved

1 Combine broth, water, chicken, celery and bay leaves in large saucepan or Dutch oven; bring to a boil over high heat. Reduce heat to low; cover and simmer 30 minutes or until chicken is tender. Remove chicken to large cutting board to cool.

2 Meanwhile, trim leeks. Cut off roots, any damaged leaves and very tough tops. Cut in half lengthwise, then cut crosswise into ¾-inch pieces. Wash well in several changes of water.

3 Add leeks, barley, salt and allspice to saucepan; cover and simmer 40 minutes or until leeks and barley are tender.

4 Remove skin and bones from chicken; cut into bite-size pieces. Add chicken to soup with prunes; simmer 3 minutes or until prunes soften. Remove and discard bay leaves.

Guinness Beef Stew

MAKES 6 SERVINGS (ABOUT 1⅓ CUPS PER SERVING)

3 tablespoons vegetable oil, divided

3 pounds boneless beef chuck roast, cut into 1-inch pieces

2 medium onions, chopped

2 stalks celery, chopped

3 tablespoons all-purpose flour

1 tablespoon minced garlic

1 tablespoon tomato paste

2 teaspoons chopped fresh thyme

1½ teaspoons salt

½ teaspoon black pepper

1 bottle (about 15 ounces) Guinness

1 cup beef broth

3 carrots, cut into 1-inch pieces

4 small turnips (12 ounces), peeled and cut into 1-inch pieces

4 medium Yukon Gold potatoes (1 pound), peeled and cut into 1-inch pieces

¼ cup finely chopped fresh parsley

1 Preheat oven to 350°F. Heat 2 tablespoons oil in Dutch oven over medium-high heat until almost smoking. Cook beef in two batches 10 minutes or until browned on all sides. Remove to plate.

2 Add remaining 1 tablespoon oil to Dutch oven; heat over medium heat. Add onions and celery; cook 10 minutes or until softened and onions are translucent, stirring occasionally. Add flour, garlic, tomato paste, thyme, salt and pepper; cook and stir 1 minute. Stir in Guinness, scraping up any browned bits from bottom of Dutch oven. Return beef to Dutch oven; stir in broth.

3 Cover; bake 1 hour. Stir in carrots, turnips and potatoes. Cover; bake 1 hour 20 minutes or until beef and vegetables are tender. Stir in parsley.

Curried Parsnip Soup

MAKES 6 TO 8 SERVINGS

3 pounds parsnips, peeled and cut into 2-inch pieces

1 tablespoon olive oil

2 tablespoons butter

1 medium yellow onion, chopped

2 stalks celery, diced

3 cloves garlic, minced

1 tablespoon salt

1 to 2 teaspoons curry powder

½ teaspoon grated fresh ginger

½ teaspoon black pepper

8 cups chicken broth

Toasted bread slices (optional)

Chopped fresh chives (optional)

1 Preheat oven to 400°F. Line large baking sheet with foil.

2 Combine parsnips and oil in large bowl; toss to coat. Spread in single layer on prepared baking sheet. Bake 35 to 45 minutes or until parsnips are tender and lightly browned around edges, stirring once halfway through cooking.

3 Melt butter in large saucepan or Dutch oven over medium heat. Add onion and celery; cook and stir 8 minutes or until vegetables are tender and onion is translucent. Add garlic, salt, curry powder, ginger and pepper; cook and stir 1 minute. Add parsnips and broth; bring to a boil over medium-high heat. Reduce heat to medium-low; cover and simmer 10 minutes.

4 Working in batches, blend soup in blender or food processor until smooth. Transfer blended soup to large bowl. Serve with toasted bread, if desired; garnish with chives.

Cod Chowder

MAKES 6 TO 8 SERVINGS (8 CUPS)

2 tablespoons vegetable oil

1 pound unpeeled red potatoes, diced

2 medium leeks, halved and thinly sliced

2 stalks celery, diced

1 bulb fennel, diced

½ yellow or red bell pepper, diced

2 teaspoons chopped fresh thyme

¾ teaspoon salt

½ to ¾ teaspoon black pepper

2 tablespoons all-purpose flour

2 cups clam juice

1 cup water

1 cup half-and-half

1½ pounds cod, cut into 1-inch pieces

1 cup frozen corn

¼ cup finely chopped fresh Italian parsley

1 Heat oil in Dutch oven or large saucepan over medium heat. Add potatoes, leeks, celery, fennel, bell pepper, thyme, salt and black pepper; cover and cook 8 minutes or until vegetables are slightly softened, stirring occasionally. Add flour; cook and stir 1 minute.

2 Stir in clam juice and water; bring to a boil over high heat. Reduce heat to medium-low; cover and simmer 10 minutes or until potatoes are tender. Remove from heat.

3 Transfer 1½ cups soup to blender or food processor; add half-and-half and blend until smooth.

4 Add cod, corn and parsley to Dutch oven; bring to a simmer over medium-high heat. Stir in blended soup mixture; cover and cook over medium heat 3 minutes or until fish is firm and opaque, stirring occasionally. Serve immediately.

Corned Beef and Cabbage Soup

MAKES ABOUT 8 SERVINGS (10 CUPS)

1 tablespoon vegetable oil

1 onion, chopped

2 stalks celery, chopped

2 carrots, chopped

2 cloves garlic, minced

4 to 5 cups coarsely chopped green cabbage (about half of small head)

1¼ pounds unpeeled Yukon gold potatoes, chopped

4 cups beef broth

4 cups water

½ cup quick-cooking barley

1 teaspoon salt

1 teaspoon dried thyme

½ teaspoon black pepper

¼ teaspoon ground mustard

12 ounces corned beef (leftovers or deli corned beef, about 2½ cups), cut into ½-inch pieces

1 Heat oil in large saucepan or Dutch oven over medium-high heat. Add onion, celery and carrots; cook 5 minutes or until vegetables are softened, stirring occasionally. Add garlic; cook and stir 1 minute.

2 Stir in cabbage, potatoes, broth, water, barley, salt, thyme, pepper and mustard; bring to a boil. Reduce heat to medium-low; cook 20 minutes, stirring occasionally.

3 Stir in corned beef; cook 10 to 15 minutes or until potatoes are tender. Add additional salt and pepper, if desired.

Split Pea Soup with Ham and Ale

MAKES 6 SERVINGS

1 tablespoon olive oil
1 cup chopped onion
½ cup chopped carrot
½ cup chopped celery
3 cloves garlic, minced
1 bay leaf
¼ teaspoon dried thyme

1 bottle (12 ounces) Belgian white ale
4 cups chicken broth
1 package (16 ounces) dried split peas, picked over and rinsed
1 pound smoked ham hocks
2 cups water

1 Heat oil in Dutch oven over medium heat. Add onion, carrot, celery, garlic, bay leaf and thyme; cook 4 to 5 minutes or until vegetables begin to soften, stirring occasionally. Add ale; bring to boil over medium-high heat. Cook 6 to 7 minutes or until beer is reduced by half.

2 Stir in broth, split peas, ham hocks and water; bring to a boil. Reduce heat to medium-low; cover and simmer 1 hour or until split peas are tender, stirring occasionally.

3 Remove ham hocks to cutting board; let stand until cool enough to handle. Remove ham from hocks. Chop ham and stir into Dutch oven. Remove and discard bay leaf.

Dublin Coddle

MAKES 6 SERVINGS

8 ounces Irish bacon*

8 pork sausages, preferably Irish bangers

3 onions, sliced

Black pepper

2 pounds potatoes, peeled and thickly sliced

2 carrots, peeled and cut into 1½-inch pieces

¼ cup chopped fresh parsley, plus additional for garnish

2 sprigs fresh thyme

3 cups chicken broth or water

Or substitute Canadian bacon or pancetta.

1 Cook bacon in Dutch oven over medium heat until crisp. Remove to paper towel-lined plate; cut into 1-inch pieces. Drain all but 1 tablespoon drippings.

2 Add sausages to Dutch oven; cook 10 minutes or until browned on all sides. Remove to paper towel-lined plate; cut into 1-inch pieces.

3 Add onions to Dutch oven; cook and stir 8 minutes or until translucent. Return bacon and sausages to Dutch oven; sprinkle with pepper. Add potatoes, carrots, ¼ cup parsley and thyme; sprinkle generously with pepper. Pour broth over vegetables; bring to a boil.

4 Reduce heat to low; partially cover and simmer 1 hour 20 minutes or until vegetables are tender. Sprinkle with additional parsley, if desired.

Pork and Cabbage Soup

MAKES 6 SERVINGS

½ pound pork loin, cut into ½-inch pieces

1 medium onion, chopped

2 slices bacon, finely chopped

2 cups beef broth

2 cups chicken broth

1 can (about 28 ounces) whole tomatoes, drained and coarsely chopped

2 medium carrots, sliced

1 teaspoon salt

1 bay leaf

¾ teaspoon dried marjoram

⅛ teaspoon black pepper

¼ medium cabbage, chopped

2 tablespoons chopped fresh parsley

1 Heat large saucepan or Dutch oven over medium heat. Add pork, onion and bacon; cook and stir until pork is no longer pink and onion is slightly tender. Drain fat.

2 Stir in beef broth, chicken broth, tomatoes, carrots, salt, bay leaf, marjoram and pepper; bring to a boil over high heat. Reduce heat to medium-low; simmer, uncovered, 30 minutes. Remove and discard bay leaf. Skim off fat.

3 Add cabbage; bring to a boil over high heat. Reduce heat to medium-low; simmer, uncovered, 15 minutes or until cabbage is tender. Stir in parsley.

Potato and Leek Soup
MAKES 6 TO 8 SERVINGS

4 cups chicken broth
3 potatoes, peeled and diced
1½ cups chopped cabbage
1 leek, diced
1 onion, chopped
2 carrots, diced
1 teaspoon salt

½ teaspoon caraway seeds
½ teaspoon black pepper
1 bay leaf
½ cup sour cream
1 pound bacon, crisp-cooked and crumbled
¼ cup chopped fresh parsley

Slow Cooker Directions

1 Combine broth, potatoes, cabbage, leek, onion, carrots, salt, caraway seeds, pepper and bay leaf in slow cooker; mix well.

2 Cover; cook on LOW 8 to 10 hours or on HIGH 4 to 5 hours.

3 Remove and discard bay leaf. Whisk ½ cup hot liquid from slow cooker into sour cream in small bowl until blended. Add sour cream mixture and bacon to slow cooker; mix well. Sprinkle with parsley.

Sausage and Bean Stew

MAKES 4 TO 6 SERVINGS

2 cups fresh bread crumbs*

2 tablespoons olive oil, divided

1 pound uncooked pork sausage, cut into 2-inch pieces

1 leek, white and light green parts only, cut in half and thinly sliced

1 large onion, cut into quarters then cut into ¼-inch slices

1 teaspoon salt, divided

2 cloves garlic, minced

½ teaspoon dried thyme

½ teaspoon ground sage

¼ teaspoon paprika

¼ teaspoon ground allspice

¼ teaspoon black pepper

1 can (28 ounces) diced tomatoes

2 cans (about 15 ounces each) navy or cannellini beans, rinsed and drained

2 tablespoons whole grain mustard

Fresh thyme leaves (optional)

To make bread crumbs, cut 4 ounces stale baguette or country bread into several pieces; place in food processor. Pulse until coarse crumbs form.

1 Preheat oven to 350°F. Combine bread crumbs and 1 tablespoon oil in medium bowl; mix well.

2 Heat remaining 1 tablespoon oil in large ovenproof skillet over medium-high heat. Add sausage; cook 8 minutes or until browned, stirring occasionally. (Sausage will not be cooked through.) Remove to plate.

3 Add leek, onion and ½ teaspoon salt to skillet; cook 10 minutes or until vegetables are soft and beginning to brown, stirring occasionally. Add garlic; cook and stir 1 minute. Add dried thyme, sage, paprika, allspice and pepper; cook and stir 1 minute. Add tomatoes; cook 5 minutes, stirring occasionally. Stir in beans, mustard and remaining ½ teaspoon salt; bring to a simmer.

4 Return sausage to skillet, pushing down into bean mixture. Sprinkle with bread crumbs.

5 Bake 25 minutes or until bread crumbs are lightly browned and sausage is cooked through. Garnish with fresh thyme.

Irish Beef Stew

MAKES 6 SERVINGS

2½ tablespoons vegetable oil, divided

2 pounds boneless beef chuck roast, cut into 1-inch pieces

1½ teaspoons salt, divided

¾ teaspoon black pepper, divided

1 medium onion, chopped

3 medium carrots, cut into 1-inch pieces

3 medium parsnips, cut into 1-inch pieces

1 package (8 to 10 ounces) cremini mushrooms, quartered

2 cloves garlic, minced

1 teaspoon dried thyme

1 teaspoon dried rosemary

2 bay leaves

1 can (about 15 ounces) Guinness stout

1 can (about 14 ounces) beef broth

1 tablespoon Dijon mustard

1 tablespoon tomato paste

1 tablespoon Worcestershire sauce

1 pound small yellow potatoes (about 1¼ inches), halved

1 cup frozen pearl onions

2 teaspoons water

2 teaspoons cornstarch

Chopped fresh parsley (optional)

1 Heat 2 tablespoons oil in Dutch oven or large saucepan over medium-high heat. Season beef with 1 teaspoon salt and ½ teaspoon pepper. Cook beef in two batches 5 minutes or until browned. Remove to plate.

2 Add remaining ½ tablespoon oil and chopped onion to Dutch oven; cook and stir 3 minutes or until softened. Add carrots, parsnips and mushrooms; cook 8 minutes or until vegetables soften and mushrooms release their liquid, stirring occasionally. Add garlic, thyme, rosemary, bay leaves, remaining ½ teaspoon salt and ¼ teaspoon pepper; cook and stir 2 minutes. Add Guinness, broth, mustard, tomato paste and Worcestershire sauce; bring to a boil, scraping up browned bits from bottom of Dutch oven. Return beef and any accumulated juices to Dutch oven; mix well.

3 Reduce heat to low; cover and cook 1 hour and 30 minutes. Stir in potatoes; cover and cook 30 minutes. Stir in pearl onions; cook, uncovered, 30 minutes or until beef and potatoes are fork-tender.

4 Stir water into cornstarch in small bowl until smooth. Add to stew; cook and stir over medium heat 3 minutes or until thickened. Garnish with parsley.

Cheesy Potato Chowder

MAKES 6 SERVINGS

1½ cups water
3 unpeeled medium red
    potatoes, cubed
1 stalk celery, sliced
1 medium carrot, chopped
¼ cup (½ stick) butter
3 green onions, sliced
¼ cup all-purpose flour
1 teaspoon salt

⅛ teaspoon black pepper
4 cups milk
2 cups (8 ounces) shredded
    American cheese
1 cup (4 ounces) shredded
    Swiss cheese
½ teaspoon caraway seeds
Oyster crackers (optional)

1 Combine water, potatoes, celery and carrot in medium saucepan.
Bring to a boil over high heat. Reduce heat to low; simmer 10 minutes
or until vegetables are tender.

2 Meanwhile, melt butter in large saucepan over medium heat. Add
green onions; cook and stir 2 minutes or until tender. Add flour, salt
and pepper; cook and stir 1 minute.

3 Add milk and potato mixture to flour mixture; cook and stir over
medium heat until bubbly. Reduce heat to low; stir in cheeses and
caraway seeds. Simmer just until cheeses are melted and soup is
heated through, stirring constantly. Serve with oyster crackers,
if desired.

Chicken, Barley and Vegetable Soup

MAKES 6 SERVINGS

½ pound boneless skinless chicken breasts, cut into ½-inch pieces

½ pound boneless skinless chicken thighs, cut into ½-inch pieces

¾ teaspoon salt

¼ teaspoon black pepper

1 tablespoon olive oil

½ cup uncooked pearl barley

4 cans (about 14 ounces each) chicken broth

2 cups water

1 bay leaf

2 cups whole baby carrots

2 cups diced peeled potatoes

2 cups sliced mushrooms

2 cups frozen peas

3 tablespoons sour cream

1 tablespoon chopped fresh dill *or* 1 teaspoon dried dill weed

1 Season chicken with salt and pepper. Heat oil in large saucepan over medium-high heat. Add chicken; cook without stirring 2 minutes or until golden. Turn chicken; cook 2 minutes. Remove chicken to plate.

2 Add barley to saucepan; cook and stir 1 to 2 minutes or until barley begins to brown, adding 1 tablespoon broth if needed to prevent burning. Add remaining broth, water and bay leaf; bring to a boil. Reduce heat to low; cover and simmer 30 minutes.

3 Add chicken, carrots, potatoes and mushrooms; cook 10 minutes or until vegetables are tender. Add peas; cook 2 minutes. Remove and discard bay leaf.

4 Top with sour cream and dill; serve immediately.

Corned Beef and Cabbage

MAKES 8 SERVINGS

3½ to 4 pounds packaged corned beef brisket

3 carrots, cut into 1½-inch pieces

2 small onions, peeled and quartered

3 stalks celery, cut into 1½-inch pieces

1 bunch fresh parsley

2 large sprigs fresh thyme

1 head green cabbage (about 2 pounds), cut into 8 wedges

1½ pounds unpeeled small red potatoes, quartered

1 cup sour cream

2 tablespoons prepared horseradish

½ teaspoon coarse salt

Chopped fresh parsley (optional)

1 Combine corned beef, carrots, onions and celery in Dutch oven. Tie parsley and thyme together with kitchen string; add to Dutch oven. Add water to cover beef by 1 inch; bring to a boil over high heat. Reduce heat to medium-low; cover and cook 2½ hours or until beef is almost tender.

2 Add cabbage and potatoes to Dutch oven; cover and cook about 30 minutes or until beef, cabbage and potatoes are tender.

3 Meanwhile, combine sour cream, horseradish and ½ teaspoon salt in medium bowl; mix well. Refrigerate until ready to serve.

4 Remove herbs from Dutch oven and discard. Remove beef to large cutting board; let stand 10 minutes. Slice beef across the grain. Arrange on serving platter with vegetables; season vegetables with additional salt to taste. Sprinkle with chopped parsley, if desired; serve with horseradish sauce.

Shepherd's Pie Potatoes

MAKES 4 SERVINGS

4 large russet potatoes (about 12 ounces each)

1½ tablespoons olive oil, divided

3 to 4 tablespoons milk

2 tablespoons butter

1 teaspoon salt, divided

½ teaspoon black pepper, divided

1 small onion, chopped

1 carrot, chopped

1 clove garlic, minced

12 ounces ground beef chuck

2 tablespoons tomato paste

1 tablespoon Worcestershire sauce

½ teaspoon ground thyme

½ cup water

½ cup thawed frozen peas

1 Preheat oven to 400°F. Scrub potatoes; prick all over with fork. Brush with 1 tablespoon oil; place on medium baking sheet. Bake about 1 hour or until fork-tender.

2 Cut ¼-inch slice from top of each potato. Scoop out flesh into medium bowl, leaving ¼-inch shells. Add 3 tablespoons milk, butter, ½ teaspoon salt and ¼ teaspoon pepper; mash until smooth, adding additional milk if necessary. Return potato shells to baking sheet.

3 While potatoes are baking, heat remaining ½ tablespoon oil in large skillet over medium-high heat. Add onion and carrot; cook 8 minutes or until vegetables are soft and beginning to brown, stirring occasionally. Add garlic; cook and stir 1 minute. Add beef; cook 5 minutes or until no longer pink, stirring to break up meat. Add tomato paste, Worcestershire sauce, thyme and remaining ½ teaspoon salt and ¼ teaspoon pepper; cook and stir 2 minutes. Stir in water. Reduce heat to medium-low; cook 10 minutes or until mixture thickens slightly, stirring occasionally. Stir in peas; cook 1 minute.

4 Divide beef mixture evenly among potato shells. Pipe or spread mashed potato mixture over beef mixture. (There may be extra mashed potatoes; serve on the side or reserve for another use.)

5 Bake 20 minutes or until top of potatoes begin to brown.

Pork Tenderloin with Cabbage and Leeks

MAKES 4 SERVINGS

¼ cup olive oil, plus additional
for pan

1 teaspoon salt

¾ teaspoon garlic powder

½ teaspoon dried thyme

½ teaspoon black pepper

1 pork tenderloin (about
1¼ pounds)

½ medium savoy cabbage,
cored and cut into ¼-inch
slices (about 6 cups)

1 small leek, cut in half
lengthwise then cut
crosswise into ¼-inch
diagonal slices

1 to 2 teaspoons cider vinegar

1 Preheat oven to 450°F. Brush large baking sheet with oil.

2 Combine salt, garlic powder, thyme and pepper in small bowl;
mix well. Stir in ¼ cup oil until well blended. Brush pork with about
1 tablespoon oil mixture, turning to coat all sides.

3 Combine cabbage and leek in large bowl. Drizzle with remaining oil
mixture; toss to coat. Spread on prepared baking sheet; top with pork.

4 Roast 25 minutes or until pork is 145°F, stirring cabbage mixture
halfway through cooking time. Remove pork to large cutting board;
tent with foil. Let stand 10 minutes before slicing. Add vinegar to
cabbage mixture; stir to blend.

Tip

If you can't find savoy cabbage, you can substitute regular
green cabbage but it may take slightly longer to cook. If the cabbage
is not crisp-tender when the pork is done, return the vegetables to
the oven for 10 minutes or until crisp-tender.

Pastrami Reuben Sandwiches with Beer Kraut

MAKES 4 SERVINGS

1 tablespoon canola oil

½ cup thinly sliced Vidalia or other sweet onion

1 cup well-drained sauerkraut

1 teaspoon sugar

½ cup beer

Unsalted butter, softened

8 slices rye bread

½ cup Russian dressing

4 slices Swiss cheese

1 pound thinly sliced pastrami

1 Heat oil in medium skillet over medium-high heat. Add onion; cook and stir 2 minutes or until slightly softened. Add sauerkraut and sugar; cook 3 minutes. Pour in beer; cook 3 minutes or until evaporated, stirring occasionally. Remove from heat.

2 Butter one side of bread slices. Place 4 slices bread, butter side down, on work surface. Spread with 1 tablespoon Russian dressing. Top with one fourth of sauerkraut mixture, 1 slice Swiss cheese and one fourth of pastrami. Spread unbuttered sides of remaining 4 slices bread with remaining Russian dressing; place butter side up on pastrami.

3 Heat large nonstick skillet over medium heat. Place two sandwiches in skillet; press firmly with spatula. Cook 3 minutes or until bread is golden. Turn; place second large skillet on top of sandwiches and press firmly. Cook 4 minutes or until golden. Repeat with remaining two sandwiches.

Steak and Mushroom Pie

MAKES 4 TO 6 SERVINGS

3 tablespoons butter, divided

1½ pounds boneless beef chuck steak, cut into 1-inch cubes

2 medium onions, chopped

3 stalks celery, cut into ½-inch slices

1 package (8 ounces) sliced mushrooms

½ teaspoon dried thyme

½ cup dry red wine

¼ cup all-purpose flour

1 cup beef broth

2 tablespoons tomato paste

1 tablespoon Dijon mustard

½ teaspoon salt

¼ teaspoon black pepper

1 refrigerated pie crust (half of 15-ounce package)

1 egg, lightly beaten

1 Spray 9- or 10-inch deep-dish pie plate or 1½-quart baking dish with nonstick cooking spray. Melt 2 tablespoons butter in large saucepan over medium-high heat. Add half of beef; cook 4 to 5 minutes or until browned, turning occasionally. Remove to plate; repeat with remaining beef.

2 Melt remaining 1 tablespoon butter in same saucepan over medium-high heat. Add onions, celery, mushrooms and thyme; cook and stir 4 to 5 minutes or until vegetables begin to soften. Add wine; cook and stir 3 to 4 minutes or until almost evaporated. Add flour; cook and stir 1 minute. Stir in broth, tomato paste, mustard and beef; bring to a boil. Reduce heat to medium-low; cover and simmer 1 hour to 1 hour 10 minutes or until beef is very tender, stirring occasionally. Remove from heat; stir in salt and pepper. Pour into prepared pie plate; let cool 20 minutes.

3 Preheat oven to 400°F. Roll out pie crust on lightly floured surface to fit top of pie plate. Place crust over filling; decoratively flute or crimp edges. Brush crust with egg; cut several small slits in top of crust with tip of knife.

4 Bake 23 to 25 minutes or until crust is golden brown. Let stand 5 minutes before serving.

Smoked Sausage and Cabbage

MAKES 4 SERVINGS

1 pound smoked sausage,
　cut into 2-inch pieces

1 tablespoon olive oil

6 cups coarsely chopped
　cabbage

1 yellow onion, cut into ½-inch
　wedges

2 cloves garlic, minced

¾ teaspoon sugar

¼ teaspoon caraway seeds

¼ teaspoon salt

¼ teaspoon black pepper

1 package (2 pounds)
　refrigerated mashed
　potatoes*

*You may substitute thawed frozen
mashed potatoes.*

1 Cook and stir sausage in large nonstick skillet over medium-high heat 3 minutes or until browned. Transfer to plate.

2 Heat oil in same skillet. Add cabbage, onion, garlic, sugar, caraway seeds, salt and pepper; cook and stir 5 minutes or until onion begins to brown. Add sausage; cover and cook 5 minutes. Remove from heat; let stand 5 minutes.

3 Meanwhile, heat potatoes in microwave according to package directions. Serve sausage mixture over mashed potatoes.

Sage-Roasted Pork with Rutabaga

MAKES 4 TO 6 SERVINGS

1 bunch fresh sage

4 cloves garlic, minced
(2 tablespoons)

1½ teaspoons coarse salt,
divided

1 teaspoon coarsely ground
black pepper, divided

5 tablespoons extra virgin
olive oil, divided

1 boneless pork loin roast
(2 to 2½ pounds)

2 medium or 1 large rutabaga
(1 to 1½ pounds)

4 carrots, cut into 1½-inch
pieces

1 Chop enough sage to measure 2 tablespoons; reserve remaining sage.
Mash chopped sage, garlic, ½ teaspoon salt and ½ teaspoon pepper in
small bowl to form paste. Stir in 2 tablepoons oil.

2 Score fatty side of pork roast with sharp knife, making cuts about
¼ inch deep. Rub herb paste into cuts and over all sides of pork.
Place pork on large plate; cover and refrigerate 1 to 2 hours.

3 Preheat oven to 400°F. Spray large roasting pan with nonstick
cooking spray. Cut rutabaga into halves or quarters; peel and cut into
1½-inch pieces. Combine rutabaga and carrots in large bowl. Drizzle
with remaining 3 tablespoons oil and sprinkle with remaining
1 teaspoon salt and ½ teaspoon pepper; toss to coat.

4 Arrange vegetables in single layer in prepared pan. Place pork on
top of vegetables, scraping any remaining herb paste from plate into
roasting pan. Tuck 3 sprigs of remaining sage into vegetables.

5 Roast 15 minutes. *Reduce oven temperature to 325°F.* Roast 45 minutes
to 1 hour 15 minutes or until pork is 145°F and barely pink in center,
stirring vegetables once or twice during cooking time. Let pork stand
5 minutes before slicing.

Tip

Rutabagas can be difficult to cut—they are a tough vegetable
and slippery on the outside because they are waxed. Cutting
them into large pieces (halves or quarters) before peeling
and chopping makes them easier to manage.

Bangers and Mash

MAKES 4 TO 6 SERVINGS

2 pounds bangers or fresh
  mild pork sausages

2 tablespoons vegetable oil,
  divided

2¼ pounds Yukon Gold
  potatoes, unpeeled and
  cut into 1-inch pieces

¾ cup milk, heated

3 tablespoons butter, melted

1½ teaspoons coarse salt

2 small yellow onions, halved
  and thinly sliced (about
  2 cups)

1 tablespoon butter

1 tablespoon all-purpose flour

¼ cup dry red wine

1¼ cups beef broth

  Additional salt and black
  pepper

1 Preheat oven to 400°F. Line baking sheet with foil. Combine sausages
  and 1 tablespoon oil in large bowl; toss to coat. Place on prepared
  baking sheet; bake 20 minutes or until cooked through and golden
  brown, turning once halfway through cooking.

2 Meanwhile, place potatoes in large saucepan; add water to cover by
  2 inches. Bring to a boil over high heat. Reduce heat to medium-low;
  cook 12 minutes or until tender. Drain well and press through ricer
  or mash with potato masher. Stir in warm milk, melted butter and
  1½ teaspoons salt until well blended. Set aside and keep warm.

3 Heat remaining 1 tablespoon oil in medium saucepan over medium
  heat. Add onions; cover and cook 20 minutes or until caramelized,
  adding ½ cup water halfway through cooking and stirring occasionally.
  Add 1 tablespoon butter; cook and stir until melted. Add flour;
  cook and stir 1 minute. Add wine; cook 30 seconds or until almost
  evaporated. Add broth; cook over medium-high heat 5 minutes or
  until thickened, stirring occasionally. Season with additional salt and
  pepper.

4 Serve bangers with mashed potatoes and onion gravy.

Ham with Dark Beer Gravy

MAKES 10 TO 12 SERVINGS

1 fully cooked bone-in ham
(about 6 pounds)

1 tablespoon Dijon mustard

2 cans (6 ounces each)
pineapple juice

1 bottle (12 ounces) dark beer,
such as porter

Dark Beer Gravy (recipe
follows)

1 Line large roasting pan with foil.

2 Remove skin and excess fat from ham. Score ham in diamond pattern.

3 Place ham in prepared pan. Spread mustard over ham. Pour pineapple
juice and beer over ham. Cover and refrigerate 8 hours.

4 Preheat oven to 350°F. Cook ham 1½ hours or until 140°F, basting
every 30 minutes. Remove ham to cutting board. Cover loosely with
foil; let stand 15 minutes before slicing.

5 Meanwhile, pour drippings from pan into 4-cup measuring cup. Let
stand 5 minutes; skim off and discard fat. Prepare Dark Beer Gravy;
serve with ham.

Dark Beer Gravy

MAKES 2½ CUPS

¼ cup (½ stick) butter

¼ cup all-purpose flour

½ cup dark beer, such as porter

2 cups drippings from roasting
pan

Salt and black pepper

Melt butter in small saucepan over medium heat. Whisk in flour
until blended. Cook 1 to 2 minutes, whisking constantly. Add beer to
drippings; whisk into flour mixture. Cook until mixture is thickened
and bubbly, whisking constantly. Season with salt and pepper.

Herbed Pork with Potatoes and Green Beans

MAKES 4 SERVINGS

2 tablespoons chopped fresh thyme

2 tablespoons chopped fresh rosemary

2 cloves garlic, minced

2 teaspoons salt

¾ teaspoon black pepper

¼ cup olive oil

1½ pounds fingerling potatoes (about 18 potatoes), cut in half lengthwise

1 pound green beans

2 pork tenderloins (about 12 ounces each)

1 Preheat oven to 450°F. Combine thyme, rosemary, garlic, salt and pepper in small bowl. Stir in oil until well blended.

2 Place potatoes in medium bowl. Drizzle with one third of oil mixture, toss to coat. Arrange potatoes, cut sides down, in rows covering two thirds of large baking sheet. (Potatoes should be in single layer; do not overlap.) Leave remaining third of baking sheet empty.

3 Roast potatoes 10 minutes while preparing beans and pork. Trim green beans; place in same bowl used for potatoes. Drizzle with one third of oil mixture; toss to coat. When potatoes have roasted 10 minutes, remove baking sheet from oven. Arrange green beans on empty third of baking sheet. Brush all sides of pork with remaining oil mixture; place on top of green beans.

4 Roast 20 to 25 minutes or until pork is 145°F. Remove pork to cutting board; tent with foil and let stand 10 minutes. Stir vegetables; return to oven. Roast 10 minutes or until golden brown. Slice pork; serve with vegetables.

Beef Pot Pie

MAKES 4 TO 6 SERVINGS

½ cup all-purpose flour

1 teaspoon salt, divided

½ teaspoon black pepper, divided

1½ pounds beef stew meat (1-inch pieces)

2 tablespoons olive oil

1 pound unpeeled new red potatoes, cubed

2 cups baby carrots

1 cup frozen pearl onions, thawed

1 parsnip, peeled and cut into 1-inch pieces

1 cup stout

¾ cup beef broth

1 teaspoon chopped fresh thyme *or* ½ teaspoon dried thyme

1 refrigerated pie crust (half of 15-ounce package)

1 Preheat oven to 350°F. Combine flour, ½ teaspoon salt and ¼ teaspoon pepper in large resealable food storage bag. Add beef; shake to coat.

2 Heat oil in large skillet over medium-high heat. Add beef; cook until browned on all sides. (Do not crowd beef; cook in batches if necessary.) Transfer to 2½- to 3-quart casserole. Stir in potatoes, carrots, onions and parsnip.

3 Add stout, broth, thyme, remaining ½ teaspoon salt and ¼ teaspoon pepper to same skillet. Bring to a boil, scraping up browned bits from bottom of skillet. Pour into casserole; mix well.

4 Cover and bake 2½ to 3 hours or until beef is fork-tender, stirring once. Uncover; let stand at room temperature 15 minutes. *Increase oven temperature to 425°F.*

5 Place pie crust over casserole and press edges to seal. Cut slits in crust to vent. Bake 15 to 20 minutes or until crust is golden brown. Cool slightly before serving.

Individual Beef Pot Pies

Instead of a refrigerated pie crust, use 1 sheet puff pastry (half of 17-ounce package). Divide beef filling among six individual ovenproof serving dishes. Cut puff pastry to fit, press over moistened edges and crimp to seal. Brush tops with 1 egg yolk, lightly beaten. Bake in preheated 400°F oven 15 to 20 minutes or until crust is puffed and golden.

Cider Pork and Onions

MAKES 8 SERVINGS

2 to 3 tablespoons vegetable oil

4 to 4½ pounds bone-in pork shoulder roast (pork butt)

4 to 5 medium onions, sliced (about 4 cups)

1 teaspoon salt, divided

4 cloves garlic, minced

3 sprigs fresh rosemary

½ teaspoon black pepper

2 to 3 cups apple cider

1 Preheat oven to 325°F. Heat 2 tablespoons oil in Dutch oven over medium-high heat. Add pork; cook until browned on all sides. Remove to plate.

2 Add onions and ½ teaspoon salt to Dutch oven; cook 10 minutes or until translucent, stirring occasionally and adding additional oil as needed to prevent scorching. Add garlic; cook and stir 1 minute. Add pork and rosemary; sprinkle with remaining ½ teaspoon salt and pepper. Add cider to come about halfway up sides of pork.

3 Cover and bake 2 to 2½ hours or until pork is very tender. (Meat should be almost falling off bones.) Remove to large platter; tent with foil to keep warm.

4 Remove and discard rosemary sprigs. Boil liquid in Dutch oven over medium-high heat 20 minutes or until reduced by half; skim fat. Season with additional salt and pepper, if desired. Cut pork; serve with sauce.

Cheddar-Beer Burgers with Bacon

MAKES 4 SERVINGS

1½ pounds ground beef

4 ounces sharp Cheddar cheese, cut into ½-inch cubes

½ cup beer

¼ cup chopped fresh parsley

1 teaspoon paprika

¾ teaspoon garlic powder

¾ teaspoon salt

¼ teaspoon black pepper

¼ cup mayonnaise

2 tablespoons ketchup

4 hamburger buns

4 lettuce leaves

4 slices tomato

8 slices pickle

4 thick slices red onion

8 slices bacon, cooked

1 Spray grid with nonstick cooking spray. Prepare grill for direct cooking over medium-high heat.

2 Combine beef, cheese, beer, parsley, paprika, garlic powder, salt and pepper in large bowl; stir to blend. Shape into four patties, making centers of patties slightly thinner than edges.

3 Grill patties, covered, 8 to 10 minutes (or uncovered, 13 to 15 minutes) to medium (160°F) or to desired doneness, turning once.

4 Meanwhile, combine mayonnaise and ketchup in small bowl. Top bottom half of each bun evenly with mayonnaise mixture, lettuce leaf, tomato slice, pickle slices, burger, onion slices and bacon; cover with top halves of buns.

Slow-Cooked Corned Beef & Cabbage

MAKES 10 SERVINGS

3½ cups Swanson® Beef Stock

¼ cup cider vinegar

2 medium onions, cut into quarters

5 medium potatoes, peeled and cut into quarters (about 5 cups)

5 medium carrots, cut into 2-inch pieces (about 2½ cups)

1 corned beef **or** beef brisket (about 3 pounds)

1 head green cabbage, trimmed and cut into 6 wedges (about 2 pounds)

Bouquet Garni

Slow Cooker Directions

1 Stir the stock and vinegar into a 6-quart slow cooker. Add the onions, potatoes, carrots, beef and cabbage. Submerge the *Bouquet Garni* in the broth mixture.

2 Cover and cook on LOW for 8 to 9 hours* or until the beef is fork-tender. Remove the *Bouquet Garni*.

Or on HIGH for 4 to 5 hours.

Bouquet Garni

Lay a 4-inch square of cheesecloth flat on the counter.
Place **4 cloves** garlic, **1 tablespoon** pickling spice and **2** bay leaves in the center of the cloth. Bring the corners of the cheesecloth together and tie with kitchen string into a bundle.

Kitchen Tip

For thicker sauce: Remove the beef and vegetables from the cooker. Stir 2 tablespoons cornstarch and 2 tablespoons water in a small bowl until smooth. Add to the cooker and cook on HIGH for 15 minutes or until the mixture boils and thickens.

Garlic Pork with Roasted Red Potatoes

MAKES 4 SERVINGS

½ teaspoon paprika

½ teaspoon garlic powder

1 pound pork tenderloin

1 tablespoon extra virgin olive oil

6 unpeeled new red potatoes, scrubbed and quartered

1 teaspoon dried oregano

½ teaspoon salt

½ teaspoon black pepper

1 Preheat oven to 425°F. Spray 13×9-inch baking pan with nonstick cooking spray.

2 Combine paprika and garlic powder in small bowl; sprinkle evenly over pork.

3 Spray large skillet with cooking spray; heat over medium-high heat. Cook pork 3 minutes per side or until browned. Place in center of prepared pan.

4 Remove skillet from heat. Add oil, potatoes and oregano; toss to coat. Arrange potato mixture around pork, scraping sides and bottom of skillet with rubber spatula. Combine salt and pepper in small bowl; sprinkle evenly over all. Bake, uncovered, 22 minutes or until pork reaches 155° to 160°F.

5 Remove pork to large cutting board; let stand 5 minutes before slicing. Stir potatoes, cover with foil and let stand while pork is resting. Serve pork with potatoes.

CHICKEN AND LAMB

Irish Stout Chicken

MAKES 4 SERVINGS

2 tablespoons vegetable oil
1 medium onion, chopped
2 cloves garlic, minced
1 cut-up whole chicken
   (3 to 4 pounds)
5 carrots, sliced
2 parsnips, sliced

1 teaspoon dried thyme
¾ teaspoon salt
½ teaspoon black pepper
¾ cup Irish stout
8 ounces sliced mushrooms
¾ cup frozen peas

1 Heat oil in large skillet over medium heat. Add onion and garlic; cook and stir 3 minutes or until tender. Remove to small bowl.

2 Add chicken to skillet in single layer; cook over medium-high heat 6 minutes per side or until browned.

3 Add onion mixture, carrots, parsnips, thyme, salt and pepper to skillet. Add stout; bring to a boil over high heat. Reduce heat to low; cover and simmer 35 minutes.

4 Add mushrooms and peas to skillet; cover and cook 10 minutes. Uncover; cook over medium heat 10 minutes or until sauce is slightly thickened and chicken is cooked through (165°F).

Rack of Lamb

MAKES 4 SERVINGS

½ cup Irish stout

2 tablespoons Dijon mustard

2 tablespoons chopped fresh parsley

2 tablespoons chopped fresh thyme

1 French cut rack of lamb (8 ribs, 1½ pounds)

½ teaspoon kosher salt

½ teaspoon black pepper

1 Position rack in center of oven. Preheat oven to 400°F. Spray broiler pan and rack with nonstick cooking spray.

2 Combine stout, mustard, parsley and thyme in small bowl.

3 Sprinkle both sides of lamb with salt and pepper; spread with stout mixture. Place lamb, bone side down, on prepared broiler pan.

4 Roast 45 minutes for medium rare (145°F) or to desired doneness. Cover with foil; let stand 10 minutes before slicing. Cut into eight pieces.

Tip

To help prevent too much browning on the tips of the bones, cover them with foil.

Simple Roasted Chicken

MAKES 4 SERVINGS

1 whole chicken (about 4 pounds)
3 tablespoons butter, softened
1½ teaspoons salt
1 teaspoon onion powder
1 teaspoon dried thyme

½ teaspoon garlic powder
½ teaspoon paprika
½ teaspoon black pepper
Fresh parsley sprigs and lemon wedges (optional)

1 Preheat oven to 425°F. Pat chicken dry; place in small baking dish or on medium baking sheet.

2 Combine butter, salt, onion powder, thyme, garlic powder, paprika and pepper in small microwavable bowl; mash with fork until well blended. Loosen skin on breasts and thighs; spread about one third of butter mixture under skin.

3 Microwave remaining butter mixture until melted. Brush melted butter mixture all over outside of chicken and inside cavity. Tie drumsticks together with kitchen string and tuck wing tips under.

4 Roast 20 minutes. *Reduce oven temperature to 375°F.* Roast 45 to 55 minutes or until chicken is cooked through (165°F), basting once with pan juices during last 10 minutes of cooking time. Remove chicken to large cutting board; tent with foil. Let stand at least 15 minutes before carving. Garnish, if desired.

Lamb and Potato Hot Pot

MAKES 4 TO 6 SERVINGS

3 tablespoons canola oil, divided

1½ pounds boneless leg of lamb, cut into 1-inch cubes

4 medium onions, thinly sliced

3 carrots, thinly sliced

1 teaspoon chopped fresh thyme

2 tablespoons all-purpose flour

1¼ cups chicken broth

¾ teaspoon salt, divided

¼ teaspoon black pepper

3 medium russet potatoes, peeled and thinly sliced

1 tablespoon butter, cut into small pieces

1 Preheat oven to 350°F. Spray 2-quart casserole with nonstick cooking spray.

2 Heat 2 tablespoons oil in large saucepan over medium-high heat. Add half of lamb; cook 4 to 5 minutes or until browned, turning occasionally. Remove to plate; repeat with remaining lamb.

3 Heat remaining 1 tablespoon oil in saucepan over medium-high heat. Add onions, carrots and thyme; cook 10 to 12 minutes or until onions are golden, stirring occasionally. Stir in lamb and any accumulated juices; cook 1 minute. Add flour; cook and stir 1 minute. Stir in broth, ½ teaspoon salt and pepper; bring to a boil and cook 1 minute or until mixture starts to thicken. Transfer to prepared casserole.

4 Arrange potato slices in overlapping layer over lamb mixture, starting from sides of casserole and working in towards center. Sprinkle potatoes with remaining ¼ teaspoon salt; dot with butter. Cover tightly with foil.

5 Bake 1 hour. Uncover; bake 15 to 20 minutes or until potatoes just begin to brown at edges and lamb is tender.

Roasted Chicken Thighs
with Mustard-Cream Sauce

MAKES 4 SERVINGS

8 bone-in skin-on chicken thighs

¾ teaspoon black pepper, divided

¼ teaspoon plus ⅛ teaspoon salt, divided

2 teaspoons vegetable oil

2 shallots, thinly sliced

½ Granny Smith apple, peeled and cut into ¼-inch pieces

½ cup chicken broth

½ cup whipping cream

1 tablespoon spicy brown mustard

½ teaspoon chopped fresh thyme

1 Preheat oven to 400°F.

2 Sprinkle both sides of chicken with ½ teaspoon pepper and ¼ teaspoon salt. Heat oil in large ovenproof skillet over medium-high heat. Add chicken, skin side down; cook 8 to 10 minutes or until skin is golden brown. Remove chicken to plate; drain excess fat from skillet.

3 Return chicken to skillet, skin side up. Transfer skillet to oven; roast 25 minutes or until cooked through (165°F). Remove chicken to clean plate; tent with foil to keep warm.

4 Drain all but 1 tablespoon fat from skillet; heat over medium heat. Add shallots and apple; cook and stir 8 minutes or until tender. Add broth; cook over medium-high heat 1 minute or until reduced by half, scraping up browned bits from bottom of skillet. Add cream, mustard, thyme, remaining ¼ teaspoon pepper and ⅛ teaspoon salt; cook and stir 2 minutes or until slightly thickened. Spoon sauce over chicken. Serve immediately.

Lamb Shanks Braised in Stout

MAKES 4 SERVINGS

4 lamb shanks, (about 1 pound each)*

¼ cup all-purpose flour

¼ cup vegetable oil, plus additional as needed

1 large onion, chopped (about 2 cups)

4 cloves garlic, minced

Salt and black pepper

3 sprigs fresh rosemary

3 sprigs fresh thyme

1 bottle (about 11 ounces) Irish stout

2 to 3 cups chicken broth

Smashed Chat Potatoes (page 105)

1 tablespoon chopped fresh mint

For a more attractive presentation, ask butcher to "french" chops by removing flesh from last inch of bone end.

1 Preheat oven to 325°F. Trim excess fat from lamb shanks. (Do not remove all fat or lamb will fall apart while cooking.) Dust lamb with flour. Heat ¼ cup oil in large roasting pan or Dutch oven over medium-high heat. Add lamb in batches; cook until browned on all sides. Remove to bowl.

2 Add oil to pan, if necessary, to make about 2 tablespoons. Add onion; cook and stir 2 minutes. Add garlic; cook and stir 2 minutes. Return lamb shanks and any accumulated juices to pan; sprinkle generously with salt and pepper. Tuck rosemary and thyme sprigs around lamb. Add stout to pan; pour in broth to almost cover lamb.

3 Cover; bake 2 hours or until lamb is very tender and almost falling off bones. Prepare Smashed Chat Potatoes.

4 Remove lamb to plate; keep warm. Skim fat from juices in pan; boil until reduced by half. Strain sauce. Serve lamb over potatoes; sprinkle with mint.

Smashed Chat Potatoes

1½ to 2 pounds unpeeled small
  white potatoes

1 tablespoon butter
Salt and black pepper

Place potatoes in large saucepan; cover with cold water by 2 inches.
Bring to a boil over high heat. Reduce heat to medium-low; simmer
20 minutes or until fork-tender. Drain potatoes; return to saucepan
and stir in butter until melted. Partially smash potatoes with fork or
potato masher. Season with salt and pepper.

Note
In Irish dialect, "chat potatoes" are small white potatoes
most often served whole and unpeeled after steaming
or boiling. Any small potato may be substituted.

Blue Cheese Stuffed Chicken Breasts

MAKES 4 SERVINGS

½ cup crumbled blue cheese

2 tablespoons butter, softened, divided

¾ teaspoon dried thyme

Salt and black pepper

4 bone-in skin-on chicken breasts

1 tablespoon lemon juice

1 Preheat oven to 400°F. Combine cheese, 1 tablespoon butter and thyme in small bowl; mix well. Season with salt and pepper.

2 Loosen chicken skin by pushing fingers between skin and meat, taking care not to tear skin. Spread cheese mixture under skin; massage skin to spread mixture evenly over chicken breasts. Place in shallow roasting pan.

3 Melt remaining 1 tablespoon butter in small bowl; stir in lemon juice until blended. Brush mixture over chicken. Sprinkle with salt and pepper.

4 Roast 50 minutes or until chicken is cooked through (165°F).

Lamb in Dill Sauce

MAKES 6 SERVINGS

2 large boiling potatoes, peeled and cut into 1-inch cubes

½ cup chopped onion

1½ teaspoons salt

½ teaspoon black pepper

½ teaspoon dried dill weed *or* 4 sprigs fresh dill

1 bay leaf

2 pounds lamb stew meat, cut into 1-inch cubes

1 cup plus 3 tablespoons water, divided

2 tablespoons all-purpose flour

1 teaspoon sugar

2 tablespoons lemon juice

Fresh dill sprigs (optional)

Slow Cooker Directions

1 Layer potatoes, onion, salt, pepper, dried dill, bay leaf, lamb and 1 cup water in slow cooker. Cover; cook on LOW 6 to 8 hours.

2 Remove lamb and potatoes to bowl with slotted spoon; cover and keep warm. Remove and discard bay leaf. Stir remaining 3 tablespoons water into flour in small bowl until smooth. Add ½ cup cooking liquid and sugar; mix well. Stir into slow cooker. *Turn slow cooker to HIGH.* Cook, uncovered, on HIGH, 15 minutes or until thickened.

3 Stir in lemon juice. Return lamb and potatoes to slow cooker. Cover; cook on HIGH 15 minutes or until heated through. Garnish with fresh dill.

Shepherd's Pie

MAKES 4 TO 6 SERVINGS

3 medium russet potatoes (1½ pounds), peeled and cut into 1-inch pieces

½ cup milk

5 tablespoons butter, divided

1 teaspoon salt, divided

½ teaspoon black pepper, divided

2 medium onions, chopped

2 medium carrots, finely chopped

½ teaspoon dried thyme

1½ pounds ground lamb

3 tablespoons tomato paste

1 tablespoon Worcestershire sauce

1½ cups beef broth

½ cup frozen peas

1 Preheat oven to 350°F. Spray 1½-quart baking dish with nonstick cooking spray.

2 Place potatoes in large saucepan; add cold water to cover by 2 inches. Bring to a boil over medium-high heat; cook 16 to 18 minutes or until tender. Drain potatoes; return to saucepan.

3 Heat milk in small saucepan over medium-high heat. Add 3 tablespoons butter, ½ teaspoon salt and ¼ teaspoon pepper; stir until butter is melted. Pour milk mixture into saucepan with potatoes; mash until smooth. Set aside.

4 Melt remaining 2 tablespoons butter in large skillet over medium heat. Add onions, carrots and thyme; cook 8 to 10 minutes or until vegetables are softened but not browned, stirring occasionally. Add lamb; cook over medium-high heat 4 minutes or until no longer pink. Drain excess fat. Return skillet to heat; cook 5 to 6 minutes or until lamb is lightly browned. Add tomato paste and Worcestershire sauce; cook 1 minute. Stir in broth; bring to a boil and cook 7 to 8 minutes or until nearly evaporated. Stir in peas, remaining ½ teaspoon salt and ¼ teaspoon pepper; cook 30 seconds. Pour mixture into prepared baking dish.

5 Spread mashed potatoes in even layer over lamb mixture; use spatula to swirl potatoes or fork to make crosshatch design on top.

6 Bake about 35 minutes or until filling is hot and bubbly and potatoes begin to brown.

Honey Lemon Garlic Chicken

MAKES 4 SERVINGS

2 lemons, divided

2 tablespoons butter, melted

2 tablespoons honey

3 cloves garlic, chopped

2 sprigs fresh rosemary, leaves removed from stems

1 teaspoon coarse salt

½ teaspoon black pepper

3 pounds chicken (4 bone-in skin-on chicken thighs and 4 drumsticks)

1¼ pounds unpeeled small potatoes, cut into halves or quarters

1 Preheat oven to 375°F. Grate peel and squeeze juice from 1 lemon. Cut remaining lemon into slices.

2 Combine lemon peel, lemon juice, butter, honey, garlic, rosemary leaves, salt and pepper in small bowl; mix well. Combine chicken, potatoes and lemon slices in large bowl. Pour butter mixture over chicken mixture; toss to coat. Arrange in single layer on large rimmed baking sheet or in shallow roasting pan.

3 Bake 1 hour or until potatoes are tender and chicken is cooked through (165°F). Cover loosely with foil if chicken skin is becoming too dark.

Roasted Dijon Lamb with Herbs and Country Vegetables

MAKES 12 SERVINGS

20 cloves garlic, peeled (about 2 medium heads)

¼ cup Dijon mustard

2 tablespoons water

2 tablespoons fresh rosemary leaves

1 tablespoon fresh thyme

1¼ teaspoons salt, divided

1 teaspoon black pepper

4½ pounds boneless leg of lamb,* trimmed

1 pound parsnips, cut diagonally into ½-inch pieces

1 pound carrots, cut diagonally into ½-inch pieces

2 large onions, cut into ½-inch wedges

3 tablespoons extra virgin olive oil, divided

If unavailable, substitute packaged marinated lamb, rinse well and pat dry.

1 Combine garlic, mustard, water, rosemary, thyme, ¾ teaspoon salt and pepper in food processor or blender; process until smooth. Place lamb in large bowl or baking pan. Spoon mixture over top and sides of lamb. Cover; refrigerate at least 8 hours.

2 Preheat oven to 500°F. Line broiler pan with foil; top with broiler rack. Coat rack with nonstick cooking spray. Combine parsnips, carrots, onions and 2 tablespoons oil in large bowl; toss to coat. Spread evenly on broiler rack; top with lamb.

3 Roast 15 minutes. *Reduce oven temperature to 325°F.* Roast 1 hour 20 minutes or until lamb is 155°F for medium or to desired doneness.

4 Transfer lamb to large cutting board; let stand 10 minutes before slicing. Continue roasting vegetables 10 minutes.

Herb Roasted Chicken

MAKES 4 SERVINGS

1 whole chicken (3 to 4 pounds)

1¼ teaspoons salt, divided

½ teaspoon black pepper, divided

1 lemon, cut into quarters

4 sprigs fresh rosemary, divided

4 sprigs fresh thyme, divided

4 cloves garlic, peeled

2 tablespoons oil

1 Preheat oven to 425°F. Place chicken, breast side up, in shallow roasting pan. Season cavity of chicken with ½ teaspoon salt and ¼ teaspoon pepper. Fill cavity with lemon quarters, 2 sprigs rosemary, 2 sprigs thyme and garlic cloves.

2 Chop remaining rosemary and thyme leaves; combine with olive oil, remaining ¾ teaspoon salt and ¼ teaspoon pepper in small bowl. Brush mixture over chicken.

3 Roast 30 minutes. *Reduce oven temperature to 375°F;* roast 35 to 45 minutes or until cooked through (165°F). Let stand 10 to 15 minutes before carving.

Sheet Pan Chicken and Sausage Supper

MAKES ABOUT 6 SERVINGS

⅓ cup olive oil

2 tablespoons balsamic vinegar

1 teaspoon salt

1 teaspoon garlic powder

½ teaspoon black pepper

¼ teaspoon red pepper flakes

3 pounds bone-in chicken thighs and drumsticks

1 pound uncooked sweet Italian sausage (4 to 5 links), cut diagonally into 2-inch pieces

6 to 8 small red onions (about 1½ pounds), each cut into 6 wedges

3½ cups broccoli florets

1 Preheat oven to 425°F. Line large baking sheet with foil, if desired.

2 Whisk oil, vinegar, salt, garlic powder, black pepper and red pepper flakes in small bowl until well blended. Combine chicken, sausage and onions on prepared baking sheet. Drizzle with oil mixture; toss until well coated. Spread meat and onions in single layer (chicken thighs should be skin side up).

3 Bake 30 minutes. Add broccoli to baking sheet; stir to coat broccoli with pan juices and turn sausage. Bake 30 minutes or until broccoli is beginning to brown and chicken is cooked through (165°F).

Honey Mustard Herbed Lamb with Vegetables

MAKES 4 SERVINGS

3 tablespoons finely chopped fresh parsley

2 tablespoons minced fresh rosemary

2 cloves garlic, minced

1¼ teaspoons salt

½ teaspoon black pepper

¼ cup olive oil

2 tablespoons honey

2 tablespoons whole grain mustard

4 lamb shoulder chops (6 to 8 ounces each)

1 pound unpeeled small red potatoes, cut into halves (or quarters if large)

1 pound unpeeled small yellow potatoes, cut into halves (or quarters if large)

1½ pounds medium carrots, peeled, cut in half lengthwise then cut into 2-inch lengths

1 Preheat oven to 425°F. Combine parsley, rosemary, garlic, salt and pepper in small bowl; mix well. Stir in oil until well blended.

2 Remove half of mixture to large shallow dish; stir in honey and mustard. Add lamb chops to dish; turn to coat both sides with mustard mixture. Set aside to marinate while preparing vegetables.

3 Combine potatoes and carrots on baking sheet. Stir remaining half of oil mixture; drizzle over vegetables and toss to coat. Cover baking sheet with foil.

4 Roast 40 minutes. Uncover; stir vegetables and roast 10 minutes. Remove baking sheet from oven; *turn oven to broil.* Arrange lamb chops over vegetables.

5 Broil 6 minutes. Turn lamb; broil 6 minutes or until medium (140°F). (Cooking time may vary depending on how quickly oven reaches broiling temperature.)

Roasted Chicken with Cabbage

MAKES 4 SERVINGS

⅓ cup olive oil, plus additional for pan

2 tablespoons red wine vinegar

2 cloves garlic, minced

1 teaspoon salt

1 teaspoon onion powder

¼ teaspoon paprika

¼ teaspoon black pepper

8 bone-in, skin-on chicken thighs (about 3 pounds)

2 large onions, cut into ½-inch slices (do not separate into rings)

1 small head green cabbage (about 2 pounds)

Chopped fresh parsley (optional)

1 Preheat oven to 425°F. Brush large baking sheet with oil.

2 Whisk ⅓ cup oil, vinegar, garlic, salt, onion powder, paprika and pepper in large bowl until well blended. Remove half of mixture to medium bowl; add chicken and turn to coat.

3 Add onion slices to large bowl with oil mixture; turn to coat. Arrange in single layer on prepared baking sheet. Cut cabbage in half through core (do not remove core). Cut each half into 1-inch wedges. Add cabbage to bowl with oil mixture; turn to coat. Arrange cabbage over onions on baking sheet. Place chicken, skin side up, on top of cabbage.

4 Roast 50 to 55 minutes or until chicken is 165°F. Remove chicken to plate; tent with foil to keep warm. Carefully drain liquid from baking sheet. Stir vegetables; roast 10 to 15 minutes or until edges begin to brown and cabbage is crisp-tender. Serve chicken with vegetables. Garnish with parsley.

Trout with Mushrooms and Potato-Parsnip Mash

MAKES 2 SERVINGS

4 medium potatoes, peeled and cut into chunks

4 medium parsnips, peeled and cut into chunks

¼ cup all-purpose flour

½ teaspoon dried thyme

¼ teaspoon salt

¼ teaspoon black pepper

2 fresh whole trout (about 12 ounces each), filleted

4 tablespoons (½ stick) butter, divided

12 ounces cremini mushrooms, sliced

¼ cup dry white or rosé wine

1 tablespoon minced fresh sage

1 Combine potatoes and parsnips in large saucepan; add cold water to cover. Bring to a boil over high heat. Reduce heat to medium-low; simmer until vegetables are fork-tender.

2 Meanwhile, combine flour, thyme, ¼ teaspoon salt and ¼ teaspoon pepper in shallow dish. Coat fillets with flour mixture; shake off excess. Heat 2 tablespoons butter in large skillet over medium-high heat. Add fish to skillet in single layer; cook 1 to 2 minutes per side or until fish begins to flake when tested with fork. Remove to plate; keep warm.

3 Add mushrooms to skillet; cook and stir 3 minutes, adding additional butter if necessary to prevent scorching. Season with salt and pepper. Add wine; cook and stir until most of liquid has evaporated.

4 Drain potatoes and parsnips; return to saucepan and mash. Stir in remaining 2 tablespoons butter and sage; season with salt and pepper. Serve fish over mashed vegetables; top with mushrooms.

Irish Whiskey Cured Salmon

MAKES 6 TO 8 SERVINGS

1 skin-on salmon fillet (1¾ pounds), pin bones removed

2 tablespoons Irish whiskey

⅓ cup packed dark brown sugar

3 tablespoons salt

Black bread or Irish soda bread (optional)

Fresh dill, crème fraîche, thinly sliced red onion and/or capers (optional)

1 Line rimmed baking sheet with plastic wrap. Rinse salmon and pat dry with paper towels. Arrange salmon, skin side down, on prepared baking sheet; brush with whiskey.

2 Combine brown sugar and salt in small bowl; rub mixture over salmon. Wrap plastic wrap securely around salmon. Top with another sheet of plastic wrap.

3 Place second baking sheet on top of salmon, then place heavy skillet or several cans on top to weigh it down. Refrigerate salmon at least 48 hours or up to 72 hours.

4 Remove top baking sheet. Unwrap salmon and rinse under cold running water to remove any remaining salt mixture. Pat dry with paper towels. Cut salmon into very thin slices; serve with bread and assorted toppings, if desired. Refrigerate leftover salmon up to 2 days.

Tip

Ask your fishmonger to remove the pin bones when purchasing the salmon. (Often this is already done, or you can remove the pin bones at home with tweezers.)

Mussels Steamed in Guinness

MAKES 2 MAIN-DISH SERVINGS

5 tablespoons butter, divided
2 stalks celery, chopped
1 medium carrot, chopped
½ cup chopped shallots
8 sprigs fresh parsley

⅔ cup Guinness
2 pounds mussels, scrubbed
   and debearded
Crusty bread

1 Melt 1 tablespoon butter in large saucepan over medium-high heat. Add celery, carrot, shallots and parsley; cook and stir 2 to 3 minutes or until vegetables begin to soften.

2 Add Guinness; bring to a boil and cook 2 minutes. Add mussels; cover and return to a boil. Cook 4 to 5 minutes or until mussels open. Uncover and cook 1 minute.

3 Remove from heat; discard any unopened mussels. Stir in remaining 4 tablespoons butter. Serve immediately in bowls with bread.

Pan-Roasted Pike with Buttery Bread Crumbs

MAKES 4 SERVINGS

6 tablespoons (¾ stick) butter, divided

2 cloves garlic, minced

⅓ cup plain dry bread crumbs

½ teaspoon salt, divided

4 tablespoons chopped fresh parsley

4 pike fillets or other medium-firm white fish (about 6 ounces each)

⅛ teaspoon black pepper

2 tablespoons lemon juice

1 Preheat oven to 400°F.

2 Melt 2 tablespoons butter in small nonstick skillet over medium-high heat. Add garlic; cook and stir 1 minute or just until lightly browned. Add bread crumbs and ⅛ teaspoon salt; cook and stir 1 minute. Transfer to small bowl; stir in parsley.

3 Melt 1 tablespoon butter in large ovenproof skillet over medium-high heat. Sprinkle fish with ¼ teaspoon salt and pepper. Add to skillet, flesh side down; cook 1 minute. Remove from heat; turn fish and top with bread crumb mixture. Transfer to oven; roast 8 to 10 minutes or until fish begins to flake when tested with fork.

4 Wipe out small skillet with paper towel; heat over medium heat. Add remaining 3 tablespoons butter; cook 3 to 4 minutes or until melted and lightly browned, stirring occasionally. Stir in lemon juice and remaining ⅛ teaspoon salt. Spoon over fish just before serving.

Pan-Fried Oysters

MAKES 4 SERVINGS

¼ cup all-purpose flour

½ teaspoon salt

¼ teaspoon black pepper

2 eggs

½ cup plain dry bread crumbs

5 tablespoons chopped fresh parsley, divided

2 containers (8 ounces each) shucked fresh oysters, rinsed, drained and patted dry *or* 1 pound fresh oysters, shucked and patted dry

Canola oil for frying

5 slices Irish bacon, crisp-cooked and chopped

Lemon wedges

1 Combine flour, salt and pepper in shallow dish or pie plate. Beat eggs in shallow bowl. Combine bread crumbs and 4 tablespoons parsley in another shallow bowl.

2 Working with one oyster at a time, coat with flour mixture, shaking off excess. Dip in eggs, shaking off excess; roll in bread crumb mixture to coat. Place coated oysters on clean plate.

3 Heat ½ inch of oil in large skillet over medium-high heat until very hot but not smoking (about 370°F). Add one third of oysters; cook about 2 minutes per side or until golden brown. Drain on paper towel-lined plate. Repeat with remaining oysters.

4 Toss oysters with bacon and remaining 1 tablespoon parsley in large bowl. Serve immediately with lemon wedges.

Roasted Salmon Fillets
with Irish Whiskey Sauce
MAKES 4 SERVINGS

4 salmon fillets (about
  6 ounces each)
½ teaspoon salt, divided
⅛ teaspoon black pepper
⅓ cup Irish whiskey
¼ cup finely chopped shallots
1 tablespoon white wine
  vinegar

½ cup whipping cream
1½ teaspoons Dijon mustard
2 tablespoons butter,
  cut into small pieces
2 tablespoons chopped
  fresh chives

1 Position rack in center of oven. Preheat oven to 425°F. Spray large rimmed baking sheet with nonstick cooking spray.

2 Sprinkle salmon with ¼ teaspoon salt and pepper; arrange on prepared baking sheet. Roast 8 to 10 minutes or until fish begins to flake when tested with fork.

3 Meanwhile, combine whiskey, shallots and vinegar in small saucepan; bring to a boil over medium-high heat. Cook 4 minutes or until liquid nearly evaporates and mixture looks like wet sand. Stir in cream and mustard; cook and stir 2 minutes or until slightly thickened. Remove from heat; whisk in butter, chives and remaining ¼ teaspoon salt.

4 Spoon sauce over salmon. Serve immediately.

Pan-Seared Scallops with Mushrooms and Leeks

MAKES 4 SERVINGS

3 tablespoons butter, divided

1½ pounds sea scallops, patted dry

½ teaspoon salt, divided

¼ teaspoon black pepper, divided

1 package (8 ounces) sliced mushrooms

3 medium leeks, white and light green parts only, cut in half crosswise and then very thinly slice lengthwise

2 cloves garlic, minced

½ cup vermouth or dry white wine

⅓ cup whipping cream

¼ cup (1 ounce) shredded Dubliner cheese

1 Melt 1 tablespoon butter in large nonstick skillet over medium-high heat. Sprinkle scallops with ¼ teaspoon salt and ⅛ teaspoon pepper. Add to skillet; cook 2 to 3 minutes per side or until browned and opaque. (Cook in batches if necessary to prevent overcrowding.) Remove scallops to plate; keep warm.

2 Melt remaining 2 tablespoons butter in same skillet over medium-high heat. Add mushrooms; cook 3 to 4 minutes or just until mushrooms begin to brown slightly. Add leeks and garlic; cook and stir 3 to 4 minutes or until leeks are tender. Add vermouth; cook 2 minutes or until almost evaporated. Stir in cream; bring to a boil and cook 1 minute. Add cheese, remaining ¼ teaspoon salt and ⅛ teaspoon pepper; cook and stir 30 seconds or until cheese is melted.

3 Return scallops to skillet; cook 1 to 2 minutes or until heated through. Serve immediately.

Dill-Crusted Salmon

MAKES 4 SERVINGS

4 salmon fillets (about 5 ounces each)

½ cup panko bread crumbs

½ cup finely chopped fresh dill

3 tablespoons mayonnaise

2 tablespoons olive oil

1 teaspoon salt

½ teaspoon red pepper flakes

1 Preheat oven to 400°F. Spray rack in roasting pan with nonstick cooking spray. Place salmon on rack.

2 Combine panko, dill, mayonnaise, oil, salt and red pepper flakes in medium bowl; mix well. Mound mixture evenly on top of salmon, pressing to adhere.

3 Bake 20 to 25 minutes or until topping is browned and fish begins to flake when tested with fork.

Pub-Style Fish & Chips

MAKES 4 SERVINGS

¾ cup all-purpose flour, plus additional for dusting fish

½ cup flat beer

Vegetable oil

3 large or 4 medium russet potatoes

1 egg, separated

Salt

1 pound cod fillets

Prepared tartar sauce

Lemon wedges

1 Combine ¾ cup flour, beer and 2 teaspoons oil in small bowl; mix well. Cover; refrigerate 30 minutes to 2 hours.

2 Peel potatoes and cut into ¾-inch sticks. Place in large bowl of cold water. Pour at least 2 inches of oil into deep heavy saucepan or deep fryer; heat over medium heat to 320°F. Drain and thoroughly dry potatoes. Fry in batches 3 minutes or until slightly softened but not browned. Drain on paper towel-lined plate.

3 Stir egg yolk into cold flour mixture. Beat egg white in medium bowl with electric mixer at medium-high speed until soft peaks form. Fold egg white into flour mixture. Season batter with pinch of salt.

4 Preheat oven to 200°F. Reheat oil in deep heavy saucepan to 365°F. Cut fish into pieces about 6 inches long and 2 to 3 inches wide; remove any pin bones. Dust fish with flour; dip fish into batter, shaking off excess. Lower carefully into oil; cook in batches 4 to 6 minutes or until batter is browned and fish is cooked through, turning once. Do not crowd saucepan. (Allow temperature of oil to return to 365°F between batches.) Drain on paper towel-lined plate; keep warm in oven.

5 Return potatoes to hot oil; cook in batches 5 minutes or until browned and crisp. Drain on paper towel-lined plate; sprinkle with salt. Serve fish with potatoes, tartar sauce and lemon wedges.

Traditional Mussels in Cream

MAKES 2 MAIN-DISH SERVINGS

2 tablespoons butter

1 medium onion, chopped

4 cloves garlic, minced

1 sprig fresh thyme

1 bay leaf

¾ cup whipping cream

¼ teaspoon salt

2 pounds mussels, scrubbed and debearded

1 tablespoon lemon juice

Crusty bread for serving

1 Melt butter in large saucepan over medium-high heat. Add onion and garlic; cook and stir 2 minutes or until garlic begins to brown slightly. Add thyme and bay leaf; cook 30 seconds. Stir in cream and salt; bring to a boil and cook 1 minute.

2 Add mussels to saucepan; cover and bring to a boil. Cook 4 to 5 minutes or until mussels open. Uncover saucepan; cook 1 minute. Remove from heat; stir in lemon juice. Discard any unopened mussels. Serve immediately in bowls with bread.

Broiled Tilapia with Mustard Cream Sauce

MAKES 4 SERVINGS

4 fresh or thawed frozen tilapia fillets (about ¾ inch thick and 4 ounces each)

Black pepper

½ cup sour cream

2 tablespoons chopped fresh dill

4 teaspoons Dijon mustard

2 teaspoons lemon juice

⅛ teaspoon garlic powder

Fresh dill sprigs (optional)

1 Preheat broiler. Lightly spray rack of broiler pan with nonstick cooking spray. Place fish on rack; sprinkle with pepper.

2 Broil 4 to 5 inches from heat 5 to 8 minutes or until fish begins to flake when tested with fork. (It is not necessary to turn fish.)

3 Meanwhile, combine sour cream, chopped dill, mustard, lemon juice and garlic powder in small bowl. Serve over warm fish. Garnish with dill sprigs.

Pan-Seared Sole with Lemon-Butter Caper Sauce

MAKES 2 SERVINGS

¼ cup all-purpose flour

½ teaspoon plus ⅛ teaspoon salt, divided

¼ teaspoon black pepper

1 pound Dover sole fillets

2 tablespoons vegetable oil

3 tablespoons butter

2 tablespoons lemon juice

2 teaspoons capers, rinsed, drained and chopped

2 tablespoons finely chopped fresh chives

1 Combine flour, ½ teaspoon salt and pepper in shallow dish or pie plate. Coat fillets with flour mixture, shaking off excess.

2 Heat oil in large nonstick skillet over medium heat. Add half of fillets; cook 2 to 3 minutes per side or until golden brown. Remove to plate; tent with foil to keep warm. Repeat with remaining fillets.

3 Wipe out skillet with paper towels. Add butter and remaining ⅛ teaspoon salt; cook 20 to 30 seconds or until melted and lightly browned. Remove from heat; stir in lemon juice and capers.

4 Drizzle sauce over fish; sprinkle with chives. Serve immediately.

Roasted Salmon with New Potatoes and Red Onions

MAKES 6 SERVINGS

¼ cup chicken broth

1 tablespoon olive or vegetable oil

1½ pounds small new potatoes, cut into halves

1 medium red onion, cut into ¼-inch-thick wedges

6 salmon fillets (4 ounces each)

¾ teaspoon salt

½ teaspoon black pepper

Fresh tarragon or dill sprigs (optional)

1 Preheat oven to 400°F. Spray large shallow roasting pan or jelly-roll pan with nonstick cooking spray.

2 Combine broth and oil in small bowl. Combine potatoes and half of broth mixture in prepared pan; toss to coat. Roast 20 minutes.

3 Add onion and remaining broth mixture to pan; toss to coat. Push vegetables to edges of pan; place salmon in center. Sprinkle salmon and vegetables with salt and pepper. Roast 10 to 15 minutes or until center of salmon is opaque and vegetables are tender. Garnish with tarragon.

Simple Baked Cod

MAKES 4 SERVINGS

4 cod fillets (about 6 ounces each)

½ teaspoon salt

¼ teaspoon black pepper

¼ cup (½ stick) butter

1 teaspoon chopped fresh thyme

2 teaspoons grated lemon peel

3 tablespoons chopped fresh parsley

1 Position rack in center of oven. Preheat oven to 425°F.

2 Spray large rimmed baking sheet with nonstick cooking spray. Arrange fish on prepared baking sheet; sprinkle with salt and pepper.

3 Bake 12 to 14 minutes or until fish just begins to flake when tested with fork.

4 Melt butter in small saucepan over medium heat. Stir in thyme and lemon peel; cook 1 minute. Remove from heat; stir in parsley. Spoon butter mixture over fish. Serve immediately.

Roast Dill Scrod with Asparagus

MAKES 4 SERVINGS

1 bunch (12 ounces) asparagus spears, ends trimmed

1 teaspoon olive oil

4 scrod or cod fillets (about 5 ounces each)

1 tablespoon lemon juice

1 teaspoon dried dill weed

½ teaspoon salt

¼ teaspoon black pepper

Paprika (optional)

1 Preheat oven to 425°F.

2 Place asparagus in 13×9-inch baking dish; drizzle with oil. Roll asparagus to coat lightly with oil; push to edges of dish, stacking asparagus into two layers.

3 Arrange fish fillets in center of baking dish; drizzle with lemon juice. Combine dill weed, salt and pepper in small bowl; sprinkle over fish and asparagus. Sprinkle with paprika, if desired.

4 Roast 15 to 17 minutes or until asparagus is crisp-tender and fish is opaque in center and begins to flake when tested with a fork.

ON THE SIDE

Lemon-Mint Red Potatoes

MAKES 4 SERVINGS

2 pounds unpeeled new red potatoes

3 tablespoons olive oil

1 teaspoon salt

¾ teaspoon Greek seasoning or dried oregano

¼ teaspoon garlic powder

¼ teaspoon black pepper

4 tablespoons chopped fresh mint, divided

2 tablespoons butter

2 tablespoons lemon juice

1 teaspoon grated lemon peel

Slow Cooker Directions

1 Coat 6-quart slow cooker with nonstick cooking spray. Add potatoes and oil; toss to coat. Sprinkle with salt, Greek seasoning, garlic powder and pepper. Cover; cook on LOW 7 hours or on HIGH 4 hours.

2 Stir in 2 tablespoons mint, butter, lemon juice and lemon peel until butter is completely melted. Cover; cook on HIGH 15 minutes to allow flavors to blend. Sprinkle with remaining 2 tablespoons mint just before serving.

Tip

Potatoes can stand at room temperature, covered, for up to 2 hours.

Braised Leeks

MAKES 4 SERVINGS

3 to 4 large leeks (1½ to 2 pounds)

¼ cup (½ stick) butter

¼ teaspoon salt

¼ teaspoon black pepper

¼ cup dry white wine

¼ cup vegetable broth

3 to 4 sprigs fresh parsley

1 Trim green stem ends of leeks; remove any damaged outer leaves. Slice leeks lengthwise up to, but not through, root ends to hold leeks together. Rinse leeks in cold water, separating layers to remove embedded dirt. Cut leeks crosswise into 3-inch lengths; cut off and discard root ends.

2 Melt butter in skillet large enough to hold leeks in single layer. Arrange leeks in skillet in crowded layer, keeping pieces together as much as possible. Cook over medium-high heat 8 minutes or until leeks begin to color and soften, turning with tongs once or twice. Sprinkle with salt and pepper.

3 Add wine, broth and parsley; bring to a simmer. Cover; cook over low heat 20 minutes or until leeks are very tender. Remove parsley sprigs before serving.

Tip

Leeks often contain a lot of embedded dirt between their layers, so they need to be washed thoroughly. It's easiest to slice up to-but not through-the root ends before slicing or chopping so the leeks hold together while washing them.

Serving Suggestion

Top the braised leeks with toasted bread crumbs, cheese or crisp crumbled bacon for an extra rich side dish.

Colcannon with Spinach and Parsnips

MAKES 4 TO 6 SERVINGS

3 medium russet potatoes (1½ pounds), peeled and cut into 1-inch pieces

3 parsnips (12 ounces), peeled and cut into 1-inch pieces

⅔ cup milk

5 tablespoons butter, plus additional for serving

¾ teaspoon salt

¼ teaspoon ground black pepper

3 cups baby spinach

1 Combine potatoes and parsnips in large saucepan; add cold water to cover by 2 inches. Bring to a boil over medium-high heat; cook 18 to 20 minutes or until tender. Drain vegetables; return to saucepan.

2 Heat milk in small saucepan over medium-high heat. Add 5 tablespoons butter, salt and pepper; stir until butter is melted.

3 Pour three fourths of milk mixture into saucepan with vegetables; mash until smooth. Stir in spinach until well blended. Add remaining milk mixture as needed to reach desired consistency. Transfer to serving dish; top with additional butter, if desired.

Tangy Red Cabbage with Apples and Bacon

MAKES 4 SERVINGS

8 slices Irish or thick-cut bacon

1 large onion, sliced

½ small head red cabbage (1 pound), thinly sliced

1 tablespoon sugar

1 Granny Smith apple, peeled and sliced

2 tablespoons cider vinegar

½ teaspoon salt

¼ teaspoon black pepper

1 Cook bacon in large skillet over medium-high heat 6 to 8 minutes or until crisp, turning occasionally. Drain on paper towel-lined plate. Coarsely chop bacon.

2 Drain all but 2 tablespoons drippings from skillet. Add onion; cook and stir over medium-high heat 2 to 3 minutes or until onion begins to soften. Add cabbage and sugar; cook and stir 4 to 5 minutes or until cabbage wilts. Stir in apple; cook 3 minutes or until crisp-tender. Stir in vinegar; cook 1 minute or until absorbed.

3 Stir in bacon, salt and pepper; cook 1 minute or until heated through. Serve warm or at room temperature.

Leek and Chive Champ

MAKES 4 TO 6 SERVINGS

3 medium russet potatoes
   (1½ pounds), peeled and
   cut into 1-inch pieces

6 tablespoons (¾ stick) butter,
   divided

2 large leeks, halved and
   sliced

½ cup milk

¼ cup chopped fresh chives

½ teaspoon salt

¼ teaspoon black pepper

½ cup prepared French fried
   onions (optional)

1 Place potatoes in large saucepan; add cold water to cover by 2 inches. Bring to a boil over medium-high heat; cook 16 to 18 minutes or until tender. Drain and return to saucepan.

2 Meanwhile, melt 2 tablespoons butter in medium skillet over medium heat. Add leeks; cook 5 to 6 minutes or until tender, stirring occasionally.

3 Heat milk in small saucepan over medium-high heat. Add 2 tablespoons butter; cook until melted. Pour milk mixture into saucepan with potatoes; mash until smooth. Stir in leeks, chives, salt and pepper; mix well.

4 Spoon into serving bowl; make large indentation in top of potatoes. Melt remaining 2 tablespoons butter; pour into indentation. Sprinkle with fried onions, if desired.

Mashed Carrots and Parsnips

MAKES 4 TO 6 SERVINGS

1 medium russet potato, peeled and cut into 1-inch pieces

3 parsnips (12 ounces), peeled and cut into 1-inch pieces

3 carrots (12 ounces), cut into 1-inch pieces

1 tablespoon honey

¼ cup (½ stick) butter, softened

½ teaspoon salt

¼ teaspoon black pepper

1 Place potato in large saucepan; add cold water to cover potato by 2 inches. Bring to a boil over medium-high heat; cook 7 minutes or until potato is partially cooked.

2 Add parsnips, carrots and honey to saucepan; return to a boil. Cook 16 to 18 minutes or until vegetables are tender. Drain vegetables; return to saucepan. Add butter, salt and pepper; mash until smooth. Serve warm.

Asparagus with No-Cook Creamy Mustard Sauce

MAKES 6 SERVINGS

2 cups water

1½ pounds asparagus, trimmed

½ cup plain yogurt

2 tablespoons mayonnaise

1 tablespoon Dijon mustard

2 teaspoons lemon juice

½ teaspoon salt

Grated lemon peel (optional)

1 Bring water to a boil in large skillet over high heat. Add asparagus; return to a boil. Reduce heat; cover and simmer 3 minutes or until crisp-tender. Drain.

2 Meanwhile, whisk yogurt, mayonnaise, mustard, lemon juice and salt in small bowl until smooth and well blended.

3 Place asparagus on serving platter; top with sauce. Garnish with lemon peel.

Stovies with Bacon

MAKES 4 SERVINGS

3 medium russet potatoes (about 1½ pounds), peeled

6 slices bacon

2 large onions, halved vertically and sliced

4 teaspoons butter

½ teaspoon salt

⅛ teaspoon black pepper

⅓ cup water

1 Place potatoes in large saucepan; add cold water to cover by 2 inches. Bring to a boil over medium-high heat; cook 15 minutes or until potatoes are partially cooked. Drain; let stand until cool enough to handle. Cut potatoes into ½-inch-thick slices.

2 Cook bacon in large skillet over medium-high heat 6 to 7 minutes or until crisp, turning occasionally. Drain on paper towel-lined plate. Chop bacon; set aside.

3 Drain all but 2 tablespoons drippings from skillet; heat over medium heat. Add onions; cook 8 to 9 minutes or until softened but not browned, stirring occasionally. Remove to small bowl.

4 Add butter to same skillet; heat over medium heat until melted. Add potatoes; sprinkle with salt and pepper. Top with onions and pour in ⅓ cup water; cover and cook 5 minutes. Stir in bacon; cook, uncovered, 10 to 12 minutes or until potatoes are tender and browned, stirring occasionally.

Cabbage Colcannon
MAKES 6 SIDE-DISH SERVINGS

1 pound new red potatoes, halved

1 tablespoon vegetable oil

1 small onion, thinly sliced

½ small head green cabbage, thinly sliced

Salt and black pepper

3 tablespoons butter

1 Place potatoes in medium saucepan; add water to cover. Bring to a boil over medium heat; cook 20 minutes or until tender. Drain well.

2 Heat oil in large nonstick skillet over medium-high heat. Add onion; cook and stir 8 minutes or until onion is lightly browned. Add cabbage; cook and stir 5 minutes or until softened.

3 Add potatoes to skillet; cook until heated through. Slightly mash potatoes. Season to taste with salt and pepper. Place ½ tablespoon slice of butter on each portion just before serving.

Parsnip Patties

MAKES 4 SERVINGS

1 pound parsnips, peeled and cut into ¾-inch chunks

4 tablespoons (½ stick) butter, divided

¼ cup chopped onion

¼ cup all-purpose flour

⅓ cup milk

2 teaspoons chopped fresh chives

Salt and black pepper

¾ cup fresh bread crumbs

2 tablespoons vegetable oil

1 Pour 1 inch water into medium saucepan; bring to a boil over high heat. Add parsnips; cover and cook 10 minutes or until fork-tender. Drain. Place in large bowl; coarsely mash with fork.

2 Melt 2 tablespoons butter in small skillet over medium-high heat. Add onion; cook and stir until translucent. Whisk in flour until bubbly and lightly browned. Whisk in milk until thickened; stir into mashed parsnips. Stir in chives; season with salt and pepper.

3 Shape parsnip mixture into four patties. Spread bread crumbs on plate. Dip patties in bread crumbs to coat all sides evenly. Place on waxed paper; refrigerate 2 hours.

4 Heat remaining 2 tablespoons butter and oil in large skillet over medium-high heat until butter is melted and bubbly. Add patties; cook 5 minutes per side or until browned.

Oven-Roasted Potatoes and Onions with Herbs

MAKES 6 SERVINGS

3 pounds unpeeled red potatoes, cut into 1½-inch pieces

1 sweet onion, such as Vidalia or Walla Walla, coarsely chopped

3 tablespoons olive oil

2 tablespoons butter, melted, or bacon drippings

3 cloves garlic, minced

¾ teaspoon salt

¾ teaspoon black pepper

⅓ cup packed chopped mixed fresh herbs, such as basil, chives, parsley, oregano, rosemary leaves, sage, tarragon and thyme

1 Preheat oven to 450°F. Line baking sheet or shallow roasting pan with foil.

2 Combine potatoes and onion on prepared baking sheet. Combine oil, butter, garlic, salt and pepper in small bowl; mix well. Drizzle over vegetables; toss to coat. Spread in single layer.

3 Roast 30 minutes. Stir vegetables; roast 10 minutes. Add herbs; toss to coat. Roast 10 minutes or until vegetables are tender and browned.

Roasted Curried Cauliflower and Brussels Sprouts

MAKES 10 SERVINGS

2 pounds cauliflower florets

12 ounces Brussels sprouts, cleaned and cut in half lengthwise

⅓ cup olive oil

½ teaspoon sea salt

½ teaspoon black pepper

2½ tablespoons curry powder

½ cup chopped fresh cilantro

1 Preheat oven to 400°F. Line large jelly-roll pan with foil.

2 Combine cauliflower, Brussels sprouts and oil in large bowl; toss to coat.

3 Sprinkle with salt, pepper and curry powder; toss to coat.

4 Spread seasoned vegetables in single layer on prepared pan. Roast 20 to 25 minutes or until golden brown, stirring after 15 minutes.

5 Remove from oven. Add cilantro; toss until blended.

Potato and Cabbage Gratin
MAKES ABOUT 8 SERVINGS

5 slices bacon, chopped

½ head savoy cabbage, cut into ¼-inch slices (about 6 cups)

1 teaspoon salt, divided

½ teaspoon black pepper, divided

2 pounds peeled Yukon gold potatoes (about 12 potatoes), very thinly sliced

3 tablespoons butter, cut into small pieces, plus additional for baking dish

1½ cups (6 ounces) shredded Irish or white Cheddar cheese, divided

¾ cup whole milk

1 Preheat oven to 375°F. Generously grease 2½- to 3-quart baking dish with butter.

2 Cook bacon in large skillet over medium-high heat until crisp. Remove to paper towel-lined plate. Drain all but 1 tablespoon drippings from skillet. Add cabbage, ¼ teaspoon salt and ⅛ teaspoon pepper to skillet; cook 12 to 15 minutes or until cabbage is crisp-tender, stirring occasionally. Reserve one third of bacon for top of gratin; stir remaining bacon into cooked cabbage.

3 Layer one third of potatoes in prepared baking dish, overlapping edges slightly. Sprinkle with ¼ teaspoon salt and ⅛ teaspoon pepper; dot with 1 tablespoon butter. Sprinkle with ½ cup cheese; top with half of cabbage mixture. Repeat layers. Top with remaining third of potatoes, ¼ teaspoon salt, ⅛ teaspoon pepper and 1 tablespoon butter. Pour milk evenly over potatoes.

4 Bake, uncovered, 30 minutes. Use flat spatula to press potatoes down into liquid. Bake 15 minutes; remove from oven and sprinkle with remaining ½ cup cheese and reserved bacon. Bake 15 minutes or until golden brown.

Red Cabbage with Bacon and Mushrooms

MAKES ABOUT 6 SERVINGS

5 slices thick-cut bacon, chopped (about 8 ounces)

1 onion, chopped

1 package (8 ounces) cremini mushrooms, chopped (½-inch pieces)

¾ teaspoon dried thyme

½ medium red cabbage, cut into wedges, cored and then cut crosswise into ¼-inch slices (about 7 cups)

¾ teaspoon salt

¼ teaspoon black pepper

⅔ cup chicken broth

3 tablespoons cider vinegar

¼ cup chopped walnuts, toasted*

3 tablespoons chopped fresh parsley

To toast walnuts, cook in small skillet over medium heat 4 to 5 minutes or until lightly browned, stirring frequently.

1 Cook bacon in large saucepan or skillet over medium-high heat until crisp. Remove to paper towel-lined plate. Drain all but 1 tablespoon drippings from skillet.

2 Add onion to saucepan; cook and stir 5 minutes or until softened. Add mushrooms and thyme; cook 6 minutes or until mushrooms begin to brown, stirring occasionally. Add cabbage, ¾ teaspoon salt and ¼ teaspoon pepper; cook 7 minutes or until cabbage is wilted.

3 Stir in broth, vinegar and half of bacon; bring to a boil. Reduce heat to low; cook, uncovered, 15 to 20 minutes or until cabbage is tender.

4 Stir in walnuts and parsley; season with additional salt and pepper, if necessary. Sprinkle with remaining bacon.

Creamy Slab Potatoes

MAKES 4 SERVINGS

¼ cup (½ stick) butter, melted
1 teaspoon salt
½ teaspoon dried rosemary
½ teaspoon dried thyme
¼ teaspoon black pepper

2½ pounds Yukon Gold potatoes (6 to 8 potatoes), peeled and cut crosswise into 1-inch slices
1 cup water
3 cloves garlic, smashed

1 Preheat oven to 500°F.

2 Combine butter, salt, rosemary, thyme and pepper in 13×9-inch baking pan (do not use glass); mix well. Add potatoes; toss to coat. Spread in single layer.

3 Bake 15 minutes. Turn potatoes; bake 15 minutes. Add water and garlic to pan; bake 15 minutes. Remove to serving plate; pour any remaining liquid in pan over potatoes.

Brussels Sprouts with Bacon and Butter

MAKES 4 SERVINGS

6 slices thick-cut bacon, cut into ½-inch pieces

1½ pounds Brussels sprouts (about 24 medium), halved

¼ teaspoon salt

¼ teaspoon black pepper

2 tablespoons butter, softened

1 Preheat oven to 375°F. Cook bacon in large cast iron skillet until almost crisp. Drain on paper towel-lined plate; set aside. Drain all but 1 tablespoon drippings from skillet.

2 Add Brussels sprouts to skillet. Sprinkle with ¼ teaspoon salt and ¼ teaspoon pepper; toss to coat. Spread in skillet.

3 Roast 30 minutes or until Brussels sprouts are browned and crispy, stirring every 10 minutes.

4 Add butter to skillet; stir until completely coated. Stir in bacon; season with additional salt and pepper.

INDEX

Acknowledgments

The publisher would like to thank the companies listed below for the use of their recipes and photographs in this publication.

Cabot® Creamery Cooperative

Campbell Soup Company

METRIC CONVERSION CHART

VOLUME MEASUREMENTS (dry)

1/8 teaspoon = 0.5 mL
1/4 teaspoon = 1 mL
1/2 teaspoon = 2 mL
3/4 teaspoon = 4 mL
1 teaspoon = 5 mL
1 tablespoon = 15 mL
2 tablespoons = 30 mL
1/4 cup = 60 mL
1/3 cup = 75 mL
1/2 cup = 125 mL
2/3 cup = 150 mL
3/4 cup = 175 mL
1 cup = 250 mL
2 cups = 1 pint = 500 mL
3 cups = 750 mL
4 cups = 1 quart = 1 L

VOLUME MEASUREMENTS (fluid)

1 fluid ounce (2 tablespoons) = 30 mL
4 fluid ounces (1/2 cup) = 125 mL
8 fluid ounces (1 cup) = 250 mL
12 fluid ounces (1 1/2 cups) = 375 mL
16 fluid ounces (2 cups) = 500 mL

WEIGHTS (mass)

1/2 ounce = 15 g
1 ounce = 30 g
3 ounces = 90 g
4 ounces = 120 g
8 ounces = 225 g
10 ounces = 285 g
12 ounces = 360 g
16 ounces = 1 pound = 450 g

DIMENSIONS

1/16 inch = 2 mm
1/8 inch = 3 mm
1/4 inch = 6 mm
1/2 inch = 1.5 cm
3/4 inch = 2 cm
1 inch = 2.5 cm

OVEN TEMPERATURES

250°F = 120°C
275°F = 140°C
300°F = 150°C
325°F = 160°C
350°F = 180°C
375°F = 190°C
400°F = 200°C
425°F = 220°C
450°F = 230°C

BAKING PAN SIZES

Utensil	Size in Inches/Quarts	Metric Volume	Size in Centimeters
Baking or Cake Pan (square or rectangular)	8 × 8 × 2	2 L	20 × 20 × 5
	9 × 9 × 2	2.5 L	23 × 23 × 5
	12 × 8 × 2	3 L	30 × 20 × 5
	13 × 9 × 2	3.5 L	33 × 23 × 5
Loaf Pan	8 × 4 × 3	1.5 L	20 × 10 × 7
	9 × 5 × 3	2 L	23 × 13 × 7
Round Layer Cake Pan	8 × 1 1/2	1.2 L	20 × 4
	9 × 1 1/2	1.5 L	23 × 4
Pie Plate	8 × 1 1/4	750 mL	20 × 3
	9 × 1 1/4	1 L	23 × 3
Baking Dish or Casserole	1 quart	1 L	—
	1 1/2 quart	1.5 L	—
	2 quart	2 L	—